CELTIC
NEEDLEPOINT

CELTIC
NEEDLEPOINT

Alice Starmore

PARKGATE
BOOKS

by Anaya Publishers Ltd, 1994
This edition published in 1998 by

Parkgate Books Ltd
Kiln House
210 New Kings Road
London SW6 4NZ
Great Britain

1 3 5 7 9 8 6 4 2

British Library Cataloguing in Publication Data:
A catalogue record for this book is available from the British Library.

ISBN 1 85585 578 X

Editor Sally Harding
Design and Typesetting Ian Muggeridge and Jo Tapper
Cover design Nigel Partridge
Still-life Photography Jon Stewart
Styling Barbara Stewart
Charts Michael Murphy, Stephen Dew and Delia Elliman
Techniques Illustrations Kate Simunek

Printed and bound in China by Sun Fung Offset Binding Company Limited.
Produced in association with the Hanway Press, London.

CONTENTS

INTRODUCTION

CELTIC ART
THE COURTING OF CONTRADICTION

The prospect that Celtic art holds for needlepoint is principally one of excitement. There is endless material here for inspiration, and at several different levels. Patterns can be isolated and used directly in your embroidery, or images and ideas can be adapted and translated into needlepoint.

HISTORIC RANGE OF CELTIC ART

The classical tradition held the high ground in European art and culture for so long, that any departure from it often had the status of a romantic revival movement. So great was the reverence for classical antiquities over all others, that when La Tène Celtic art objects began to be unearthed in Switzerland in large quantities during the last century, many experts were convinced that they could not be Celtic at all. An illiterate barbarian society composed of a collection of warring tribes was not considered capable of producing items of such beauty and sophistication.

Before considering the nature of Celtic art itself, it is useful to dwell upon the broad sweep of its historic range, which cannot fail to impress. Never achieving nationhood, the Celts remained a collection of tribes whose rise and fall spanned more than a millennium – from the pagan to the Christian era. From about 700 B.C. the Celtic tribes, originating in Eastern Europe, began to spread westwards through Austria, France and the Low Countries and only reached Britain and Ireland in about 250 B.C. Our knowledge of them is based on Greek, Roman and Etruscan accounts and on artefacts from archaeological sites.

Archaeologists describe the development of Celtic society in terms of the place names of important finds. Thus, the Hallstatt phase does not mean that Hallstatt – in Austria – was the centre of the Celtic universe, although large amounts of archaeological material were found there. It refers to Celtic society between about 700 B.C. and 500 B.C., when it had emerged from primitive nomadism to a society of farming, trading people, with fixed settlements and a definite social organisation.

Similarly La Tène, in Switzerland, is used to refer to the mature phase from 500 B.C. onwards, when the Celts were established as a vigorous civilisation, with a wealthy ruling class who commissioned sophisticated pieces of art from elite craftsmen. The La Tène reached the zenith of their power and glory around 200 B.C., before entering an inexorable decline, the cause of which can be summed up in one word – Rome.

While incorporating loan elements from various cultures, Celtic art maintains a distinct sense of continuity, never losing sight of its own remarkable identity. There is a definite development of sophistication over the centuries, with the Hallstatt pieces showing vigour rather than the assured delicacy of the La Tène objects and those of later phases. There is also a decided shift in purpose in Celtic art, from the aggrandisement of pagan chieftains by the display of fine weapons and drinking vessels, to the devoted glorification of Christ. Yet throughout it all, the vision remains the same.

THE VISION OF CELTIC ART

The vision of Celtic art is paradoxical. It has one eye focused on the natural world, while the other scans an abstract, inner universe with a geometric sense that some modern viewers find alien, or even unsettling. It is finely balanced on the border between these two worlds, drawing inspiration from both, while never letting one outweigh the other. The instinctive precision of this balance is the main hallmark of Celtic art, and can be demonstrated by considering the following examples of Celtic metalwork, separated by centuries but united by that common vision.

BASSE-YUTZ FLAGONS

The Basse-Yutz flagons (opposite page, top left) were unearthed in the Moselle region of France, and are luxury pieces made to grace the table of a Celtic chieftain in the first half of the fourth century B.C. Their workmanship – in bronze, coral and enamel – is masterly, and while their general line testifies to cultural influences gained through the Mediterranean wine trade, the same cannot be said of the ornamentation. On the spout of each jug swims a plump, innocent little duck, happily oblivious to the three stalking carnivores which have emerged from a stylised nightmare. The beasts are real, but they are also abstract. The largest of

Basse-Yutz flagon (one of a pair), fourth century B.C.

Coin of Apollo, second century B.C.

the three is about to pounce, but its back is extended into a graceful handle, by means of which the wine is poured. Its ears, head and deadly fangs are formed from just one sinuous line.

The jugs epitomise elegance while quietly exuding an aura of power and threat. The flagons' perfect poise depicts a dynamic, decisive moment, redolent with tension. Their owner must have been someone sophisticated enough to appreciate this tension, and the effect would surely not have been lost upon guests at the table. That decisive moment has survived two and a half millennia. The duck is still swimming and the beasts are still just about to pounce. Their creator would be amused.

COIN OF APOLLO

Made two centuries later than the Basse-Yutz flagons, the small gold coin depicting the head of Apollo (above right) comes from Northern Gaul and so represents another loan from the Mediterranean. Unlike a Roman depiction, however, the sun god's face has been relegated to the extreme edge of the coin, and occupies only a small portion of the total area. The image is dominated by the laurelled hair, swirling in a mass of shade and highlights, enhanced by the use of gold as a medium.

Hair was important to the Celts, and they took immense trouble over it. A Roman historian described Boudicca's bright red hair falling down to her knees. The pictorial emphasis on the hair of Apollo rather than on his face is therefore typically Celtic, and so is

the treatment of the image. The hair has almost been reduced to a geometric pattern, and the same is true of the god's profile. The "almost" is of vital importance. Nature is on the point of falling into total abstraction, but does not quite go over the edge. An impressionist view of nature still remains.

BRONZE CHARIOT FITTING

This impressionist view of nature can also be seen in the chased bronze chariot fitting (below) found in Britain in Stanwick, North Yorkshire, territory of the

Bronze chariot fitting, first century A.D.

Brigante tribe in the first century A.D.

The horse depicted on the flagon has been distilled to its merest essence, but a horse it undoubtedly remains. Again, we see an ambiguous entity, elegant and aloof, yet sinister and full of threat. The effect is produced by just two continuous lines that look as if they were drawn by a confident hand in a single, sweeping movement. This fluidity almost makes one doubt the solidity of the metal, and adds to the object's dream-like power.

CELTIC ART AT ITS PEAK

Finally, we cross hundreds of years to the twelfth century A.D. Most of the remaining examples of Celtic art from this period come from Ireland – the last, westernmost bastion of Celtic culture to be swamped by Romanised Europe. Ironically, the twilight of the Celts brought forth not a last dying note from their art, but a magnificent crescendo.

Twelfth-century Celtic metalwork sometimes displays Scandinavian influence, but at the same time it demonstrates Celtic art at its peak, with all the features of the past centuries brought together. The curving La Tène forms had evolved into trumpet spirals and complex interlacings. The animal forms from this period are the cousins of the beasts on the Basse-Yutz flagons. Over that tract of time, the terms of reference had remained the same, and of course, the ambiguities flowed. Nature can still be seen to be breaking down into abstruse Celtic geometry.

Above all however, is the fact that the Celtic Christian pieces of the twelfth century A.D. are as resolutely pagan as any of their Celtic forebears from the centuries B.C. Accurate observation from nature can be seen in these works sitting literally cheek by jowl with stylised abstraction.

COMMON DENOMINATORS OF CELTIC ART

Surveying these pieces of metalwork that are separated by centuries, the common denominators of Celtic art become clear.

Firstly, there is *breathtaking craftsmanship*. These are no naive pieces of folk art, but superb, sophisticated examples that could easily command respect in any place and any era.

Celtic society was sufficiently structured to allow the existence of an elite group of metalworkers with a priest-like status, which leads to the second common factor. The skill of these metalworkers produced objects with an *aura of mysticism* discernible today, and which must have verged on the supernatural during their own period.

Thirdly, there is a *repetition of image* that must have had a significance which we can only guess at. That repetition is based upon the fourth point – a *fluidity of line* which becomes more complex down the centuries, but which is never lost.

Then there are the *layers of ambiguity*, typified by the balance between nature and abstraction. In all the Celtic pieces surveyed, we see the deliberate courting of contradiction, which can unsettle, astonish, or amuse, but which can never be viewed without a sense of admiration.

The Celts were indeed an illiterate people, but they had a complex visual language of great power and subtlety, and their craftsmen used its esoteric devices in an manner as accomplished as any poet. The full impact of their metaphors is sadly lost today, unless they pluck some distant ancestral chord.

THE FINAL FLOURISH OF CELTIC ART

Celtic visual language, and the artistry behind it, were over-run and deadened by the spread of the Roman Empire. As tribes were conquered, their aristocracy were no longer in a position to place commissions, or to support metalworkers as part of their retinue, and Celtic art began to fade.

This process of the decline of Celtic influence reached Britain later than continental Europe, and the Celtic tradition survived longer, only to be modified by a Germanic overlay as the legions left and successive waves of Anglo-Saxon colonists took their place. In unconquered Ireland however, Celtic art absorbed these new borrowings without detriment, and as mentioned previously, the early centuries of Christianity saw a final flourish and a brand new medium – the illuminated manuscript.

Origins of the Book of Kells

The most famous example of the Celtic illuminated manuscript is the Book of Kells, now housed in the library of Trinity College, Dublin. This Latin text of the four gospels is generally accepted to be the one stolen from the monastery church of Colmcille, at Kells in Ireland. There is disagreement as to whether it is a product of the late eighth or early ninth century, and there is similar disagreement as to which monastic scriptorium – in Ireland or northern Britain – produced it. Certainly, it came from a centre of calligraphic and artistic expertise, for its 680 surviving pages are majestic in both text and illustration (right).

The Book of Kells was made for ceremony and worship in a Christian church, but its inspiration stems from centuries of an entirely pagan artistic tradition. Every facet of that tradition is given a final sheen; every edge of ambiguity is sharpened to ultimate perfection.

Artistry of the Book of Kells

In the Book of Kells, abstract interlacings might explode into heads or faces, but nature is never allowed to dominate. Beasts, birds and butterflies are stretched and stylised; human arms and legs are woven into knotwork patterns. There is humour here, for things appear to have been sneaked onto the page. Individuals and groups of figures peer out, sometimes morose, sometimes grumpy, and sometimes grinning smugly, perhaps at some private joke.

The artistry evident in the Book of Kells is consummate. There are details so minute as to be staggering, and although we cannot be sure of the exact techniques used, brushes of a single animal hair and a magnifying lens formed from a water drop have been suggested. Total mastery of technique caused a spontaneous flow rather than rigid formality. There is the feeling that the art poured from the artists, for there is flexibility and constant movement. Although the basic structure of a page was probably planned from the beginning, the details must have been added at will. The artists understood the underlying conceptual framework so well that they could create many variations within the same structure, and fill any type of

The Evangelists' Symbols, St. John's Gospel from the Book of Kells, Trinity College Dublin.

space. Thus we see borders within borders and shapes within shapes. We see anarchy and order in yet another seeming contradiction. This devotional work, symbolic of the ordered world of Roman Christianity, seethes with the greatest doodles known to man.

Working in the Spirit of Celtic Art

Two of the needlepoint designs in the following pages – the *Lion Tile Cushion* and the *Eagle Tile Cushion* – are faithful copies from details of a page in the Book of Kells. However, in most of my needlepoints, I have worked within the spirit of Celtic art, using its visual language to produce new, original designs. That spirit and the excitement it generated for me, is the theme of this book.

KEY PATTERNS

KEY PATTERN CUSHION

Key patterns are one of the fundamental forms
employed in Celtic decoration. The strict geometry
of the patterns is based on a system developed from
the basic square. Within the square, diagonal lines
are drawn in a particular order to create labyrinth
pathways of varying complexity. The key pattern
on the Key Pattern Cushion, composed of sixteen
patterned squares, is a fine example of the form.
I wanted to contrast the strong and rigid nature of
the pattern with soft colours, shaded at random,
so that the whole effect was one of contained
movement.

KEY PATTERN CUSHION

SIZE OF NEEDLEPOINT

The finished needlepoint cushion/pillow measures 49cm/19¼in square.

MATERIALS

10-mesh single-thread canvas 63cm/24½in square

❖

Size 18 tapestry needle

❖

Fabric for backing (and if desired, for piping/cording) and matching sewing thread

❖

2.2m/2½yd of ready-made cord or piping/filling cord

❖

46cm/18in zipper

❖

Cushion pad/pillow form 50cm/19½in square

❖

APPLETON Crewel Wool (or PATERNA/YAN Persian Yarn) in the following 12 colours:

A = brown-olive
Ap 313 (or Pa 750) 182m/200yd

B = dark gold
Ap 475 (or Pa 700) 182m/200yd

C = gold
Ap 695 (or Pa 732) 182m/200yd

D = mid mauve
Ap 604 (or Pa 322) 22m/24yd

E = light mauve
Ap 603 (or Pa 323) 22m/24yd

F = wine red
Ap 713 (or Pa 922) 91m/100yd

G = bright rose pink
Ap 223 (or Pa 931) 91m/100yd

H =mid green
Ap 544 (or Pa 692) 91m/100yd

I = light green
Ap 543 (or Pa 693) 91m/100yd

J = pale grey-green
Ap 351 (or Pa 605) 364m/400yd

K = pale yellow
Ap 692 (or Pa 744) 364m/400yd

L = ecru
Ap 691 (or Pa 645) 364m/400yd

❖

Note: For another alternative yarn brand see *Yarn Alternatives Table* on page 126. Hank and skein sizes are also given on page 126.

COLOUR MIXTURES

The embroidery for this design is worked using three strands of Appleton crewel yarn (or three strands of Paterna/yan Persian yarn). To achieve subtle shading the colours are used singly or in combination. The colour key gives the colour combinations: for example, AAB means two strands of brown-olive and one strand of dark gold used together, DDD means three strands of mid mauve used together, and so on.

WORKING THE EMBROIDERY

The design covers an area 193 stitches wide by 193 stitches tall. (The chart shows only one quarter of the cushion design.) Mark the outline of lower right-hand corner of the design (and the grid lines of the chart) onto the canvas, allowing for 6.5cm/2½ in of un-worked canvas along the two outer edges of the design. If desired, stretch the canvas onto an embroidery frame. (The technical chapter beginning on page 114 gives detailed instructions for marking the canvas, stitching and finishing your needlepoint.)

Using three strands of Appleton crewel yarn (or three strands of Paterna/yan Persian yarn) in the combinations given in the colour key, work the design in tent stitch following the chart as explained below.

Shading the patterns

Filling in the lower right-hand corner of the design, begin by working the key pattern outlines in the golden shades (AAB, BBC and CCB). It is not necessary to follow the chart square for square for the shading as long as the shades are sprinkled together in the same manner.

After completing the key pattern outlines, work the

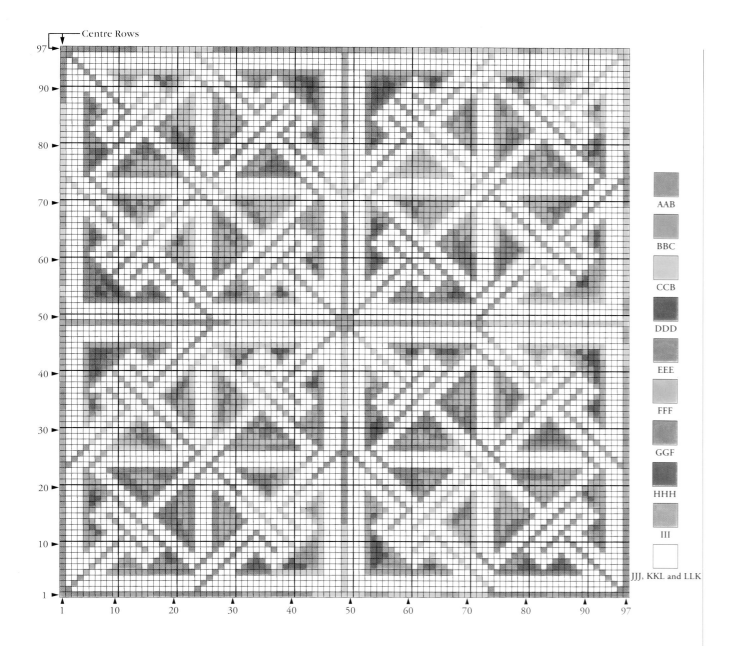

Centre Rows

AAB
BBC
CCB
DDD
EEE
FFF
GGF
HHH
III
JJJ, KKL and LLK

remainder of the design in the lower right-hand corner, with the exception of the background.

Rotating the chart

Next, turn the chart 90 degrees clockwise, keeping the centre rows in the centre so that the left edge of the chart is at the top. With the chart in this position, it now represents the design in the lower left-hand corner of the cushion. Fill in the design in the lower left-hand corner with the exception of the background, omitting the one central row of the chart which has already been filled in.

When this is complete, turn the chart 90 degrees clockwise again and work the upper left-hand corner of the design, omitting the one central row of the chart which has already been filled in. Turn the chart another 90 degrees for the upper right-hand corner.

Shading the background

Work the entire embroidery as directed above, before filling in the background. Fill in the background by working JJJ, KKL and LLK at random in the remaining areas.

Because the outer row around the perimeter of the needlepoint may be caught up in the seam, it is best to work one final row of stitches all around the outer edge, using AAB, BBC and CCB at random.

BLOCKING AND FINISHING

When the embroidery has been completed, block the canvas as instructed on page 124.

Trim the unworked canvas to about 2cm/¾ in all around the edge. Using the blocked canvas as your template, cut two pieces of backing fabric and complete as instructed on page 125.

KEY PATTERN
GLASSES CASE

The faded and patchy colours of the artwork in the Book of Kells, an inevitable consequence of the passing centuries, inspires me as much as the colours themselves. With this design I wanted to create a quick and easy project which focuses on the subtle effect of random shading. The chevron arrowhead key pattern, which comes from the Nigg Stone in northeastern Scotland, provided a simple, repetitive backdrop on which to play with this idea. I have used two threads of stranded Persian yarn and mixed the shades in both background and pattern colours.

18

KEY PATTERN
GLASSES CASE

SIZE OF NEEDLEPOINT

The finished glasses case measures 7.5cm/3in wide by 17cm/6¾in long.

MATERIALS

10-mesh double-thread canvas 20.5cm/8in by 51cm/20in

❖

Size 18 tapestry needle

❖

Small amount of lining fabric and matching sewing thread

❖

PATERNA/YAN Persian Yarn in the following 8 colours:

A = orange
Paterna shade 862 – 2 skeins

B = dusky pink
Paterna shade 922 – 2 skeins

C = pale green
Paterna shade 605 – 1 skein

D = light green
Paterna shade 604 – 1 skein

E = yellow-green
Paterna shade 644 – 1 skein

F = bright lavender
Paterna shade 323 – 1 skein

G = pale mauve
Paterna shade 256 – 1 skein

H = light lavender
Paterna shade 324 – 2 skeins

❖

Note: For yarn buying information see page 126.

COLOUR MIXTURES

The embroidery for this design is worked using two strands of Paterna/yan Persian yarn. To achieve subtle shading the colours are used singly and in combination. The colour key gives the colour combinations: for example, AA means two strands of orange used together, AB means one strand of orange and one strand of dusky pink used together, and so on.

WORKING THE EMBROIDERY

The design covers an area 31 stitches wide by 147 stitches long. Mark the outline of the design (and the grid lines of the chart) onto the canvas, allowing for 6.5cm/2½in of unworked canvas all around the design. If desired, stretch the canvas onto an embroidery frame. (The technical chapter beginning on page 114 gives detailed instructions for marking the canvas, stitching and finishing your needlepoint.)

The chart for the glasses case is illustrated in two separate sections, but the design should be worked in a continuous strip. Using two strands of Paterna/yan Persian yarn in the combinations given in the colour key, work the design in tent stitch following the chart as explained below.

Shading

It is not necessary to follow the chart square for square for the shading as long as the shades are sprinkled together in the same manner (see page 123).

BLOCKING AND FINISHING

When the embroidery has been completed, block the canvas as instructed on page 124. Be sure to allow the needlepoint to dry completely before removing it from the blocking board.

Trim the unworked canvas to about 1.5cm/½in all around the edge of the needlepoint. Cut a piece of lining the same width as the trimmed canvas but 3cm/1in shorter.

Turn under the canvas along the long sides of the needlepoint, folding along the first canvas thread (not along the holes). Then fold the needlepoint in half along chart row 74, so that the wrong sides of the needlepoint are facing and the canvas holes at the edges are lined up row for row. Using two strands of colour F and the tapestry needle, join the side seams with tent stitch.

Fold the lining fabric in half and sew the side seams 1.5cm/⅝in from the raw edge, using either backstitch or a sewing machine.

Turn the lining right side out, fold the top of the lining to the wrong side 1.5cm/⅝ in from the edge and press along the fold line.

Slip the top of the lining over the unworked canvas at the top of the needlepoint, and pin in place with the fold line of the lining along the edge of the tent stitches. Sew the lining to the needlepoint.

Push the lining into the glasses case, folding the last five rows of the needlpoint into the inside of the case.

Then work a few stitches inside the case at each side seam 1.5cm/⅝ in below the top edge to secure the lining in position.

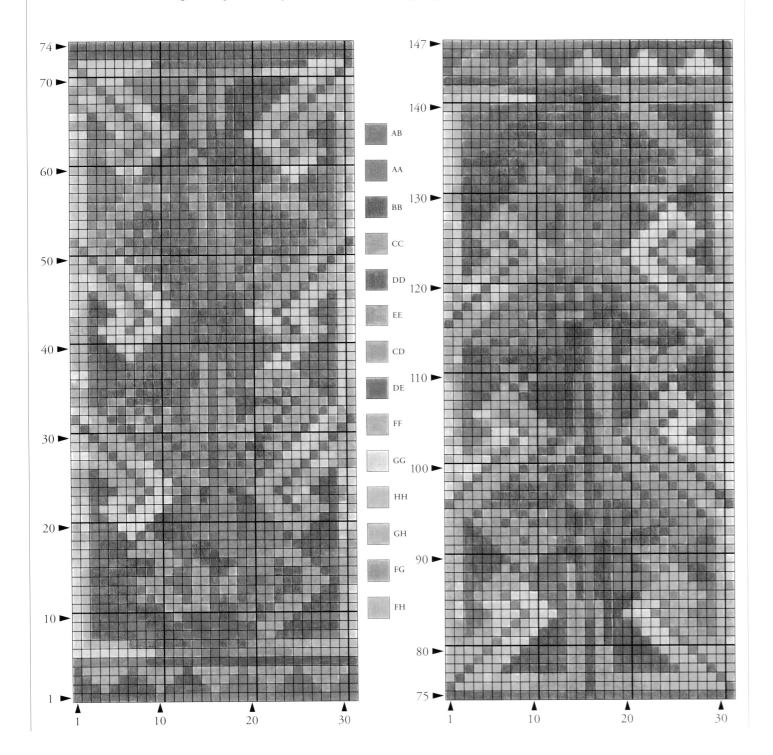

KEY AND KNOTWORK WORKBOX COVER

In Celtic artwork, key patterns were often used as borders, backdrops and fillers within more complex designs. I used this idea to create this key and knotwork design. I first charted a key pattern from the Book of Kells and then removed diamond shaped sections which I filled with a simple knotwork motif. Working directly from such an astonishingly beautiful manuscript made me wonder about the lives of the people who so painstakingly created them all those centuries ago. These thoughts inspired the idea of "painting" this pattern with venerable old golds and verdigris on a dark and mysterious blue-green background.

KEY AND KNOTWORK
WORKBOX COVER

SIZE OF NEEDLEPOINT

The finished needlepoint measures 35cm/13¾in square and can be made into a workbox cover or, if desired, a cushion/pillow cover.

MATERIALS

10-mesh single-thread canvas 48cm/19in square

Size 18 tapestry needle

APPLETON Crewel Wool (or PATERNA/YAN Persian Yarn) in the following 5 colours:

*A = dark green-blue
Ap 327 (or Pa 510) 364m/400yd*

*B = mid green-blue
Ap 157 (or Pa 532) 364m/400yd*

*C = light brown-olive
Ap 312 (or Pa 752) 182m/200yd*

*D = mid brown-olive
Ap 313 (or Pa 751) 364m/400yd*

*E = dark brown-olive
Ap 314 (or Pa 750) 182m/200yd*

Note: For another alternative yarn brand see *Yarn Alternatives Table* on page 126. Hank and skein sizes are also given on page 126.

COLOUR MIXTURES

The embroidery for the *Key and Knotwork Workbox Cover* is worked using three strands of Appleton crewel yarn (or three strands of Paterna/yan Persian yarn). To achieve subtle shading the colours are used singly or in combination.

The colour key gives the colour combinations: for example, DDE means two strands of mid brown-olive and one strand of dark brown-olive used together, AAA means three strands of dark green-blue used together, BBB means three strands of mid green-blue used together, and so on. (See pages 26 and 27 for the chart for this design.)

WORKING THE EMBROIDERY

The design covers an area 138 stitches wide by 138 stitches tall. Mark the outline of the design (and the grid lines of the chart) onto the canvas, allowing for 6.5cm/2½in of unworked canvas all around the design. If desired, stretch the canvas onto an embroidery frame. (The technical chapter beginning on page 114 gives detailed instructions for marking the canvas, stitching and finishing your needlepoint.)

Using three strands of Appleton crewel yarn (or three strands of Paterna/yan Persian yarn) in the combinations given in the colour key, work the design in tent stitch. Leaving the background until last, begin by working the key and knotwork patterns, shading as explained below.

Shading the patterns

When embroidering the key patterns and the knotwork insets, first work random streaks of colours DDC and DDE.

Shading the backgrounds

On the background around the key patterns and around the knotwork insets, work random streaks of AAA and BBB.

BLOCKING AND FINISHING

When the embroidery has been completed, block the canvas as instructed on page 124. Be sure to allow the needlepoint to dry completely before removing it from the blocking board.

If you are having the needlepoint stretched onto a workbox, do not trim the canvas as this should be left to the furniture maker making the workbox.

Making a cushion cover

If you are making the workbox cover into a cushion/pillow cover, you will need to purchase fabric for backing, matching sewing thread, a cushion pad/pillow form the same size as the blocked needlepoint and, if desired, a ready-made cord for edging. You will also need a zipper 3cm/1in shorter than the width of the finished cushion/pillow cover.

After blocking, trim the unworked canvas to about 2cm/¾in all around the edge of the needlepoint.

Using the blocked and trimmed needlepoint as your template, cut two pieces of backing fabric each half the size of the trimmed canvas and with an extra seam allowance of 2cm/¾in at the centre edge.

Insert the zipper between the two pieces of backing fabric as instructed on page 125.

Complete the backing as instructed on page 125 and sew on the ready-made cord.

AAA and BBB

DDC and DDE

70　　80　　90　　100　　110　　120　　130　　138

27

KEY AND KNOTWORK FOOTSTOOL COVER

This design is the result of a blend of inspirations, patterns and colours. My original idea was to combine two very different but constant sources of inspiration – Celtic art, and the colours and textures of the seashore. The central key pattern is rendered in a random mix of three bright colours on a mixed and muted background, suggestive of bright water moving over pebbled beaches. The knotwork border reminded me of the graceful flowing motion of seaweed on the tide, and so I accentuated this strong sense of movement by working the knotwork strands in the three solid pattern colours.

KEY AND KNOTWORK FOOTSTOOL COVER

SIZE OF NEEDLEPOINT

The finished needlepoint measures 50cm/19½in by 39cm/15½in tall and can be made into a footstool cover or, if desired, a cushion/pillow cover.

MATERIALS

10-mesh single-thread canvas 63cm/24½in 52cm/20½in

Size 18 tapestry needle

APPLETON Crewel Wool (or PATERNA/YAN Persian Yarn) in the following 6 colours:

A = *hyacinth blue*
Ap 894 (or Pa 342) 455m/500yd

B = *mauve*
Ap 453 (or Pa 301) 182m/200yd

C = *green-blue*
Ap 565 (or Pa 502) 182m/200yd

D = *light drab green*
Ap 332 (or Pa 643) 364m/400yd

E = *pale grey-green*
Ap 351 (or Pa 605) 364m/400yd

F = *light grey-green*
Ap 641 (Pa 604) 364m/400yd

Note: For another alternative yarn brand see *Yarn Alternatives Table* on page 126. Hank and skein sizes are also given on page 126.

COLOUR MIXTURES

The embroidery for this design is worked using three strands of Appleton crewel yarn (or three strands of Paterna/yan Persian yarn). To achieve subtle shading the colours are used singly or in combination.

The colour key gives the colour combinations: for example, BBA means two strands of mauve and one strand of hyacinth used together, CCC means three strands of green-blue used together, and so on. (See pages 32 and 33 for the chart for this design.)

WORKING THE EMBROIDERY

The design covers an area 195 stitches wide by 156 stitches tall. Mark the outline of the design (and the grid lines of the chart) onto the canvas, allowing for 6.5cm/2½in of unworked canvas all around the design. If desired, stretch the canvas onto an embroidery frame. (The technical chapter beginning on page 114 gives detailed instructions for marking the canvas, stitching and finishing your needlepoint.)

Using three strands of Appleton crewel yarn (or three strands of Paterna/yan Persian yarn) in the combinations given in the colour key, work the design in tent stitch. Leaving the background until last, begin by working the knotwork border pattern and the central key pattern, shading as explained below.

Shading the patterns

Work the knotwork border pattern in AAA, BBB and CCC as shown on the chart.

The central key pattern is worked with seven shades created by mixing yarns A, B and C. When embroidering the key pattern, work random streaks of AAA, BBB, CCC, AAB, BBA, AAC and CCA.

There is no need to follow the chart square for square for this shading as long as the shades are sprinkled together in the same manner (see page 123).

Note that mauve and green-blue always shade through to hyacinth blue and the mauve and green-blue are not shaded together or used next to each other on the central key pattern.

Shading the background

Work the background for the knotwork border in DEF only.

The background for the central key pattern, is worked with nine shades created by mixing yarns D, E and F. When embroidering this background, work random streaks of DDD, EEE, FFF, DDE, DDF, EED, EEF, FFD and FFE.

BLOCKING AND FINISHING

When the embroidery has been completed, block the canvas as instructed on page 124. Be sure to allow the needlepoint to dry completely before removing it from the blocking board or it may distort again.

If you are having the needlepoint stretched onto a stool, do not trim the canvas as this should be left to the furniture maker making the stool.

Making a cushion cover

If you are making the footstool cover into a cushion/pillow cover, you will need to purchase fabric for backing, matching sewing thread, a cushion pad/pillow form the same size as the blocked needlepoint and, if desired, a ready-made cord for edging. You will also need a zipper 3cm/1in shorter than the width of the finished cushion/pillow cover.

After blocking, trim the unworked canvas to about 2cm/¾in all around the edge of the needlepoint.

Using the blocked needlepoint as your template, cut two pieces of back fabric each half the size of the trimmed canvas and with an extra seam allowance of 2cm/¾in at the centre edge.

Insert the zipper between the two pieces of backing fabric as instructed on page 125.

Complete the backing as instructed on page 125 and sew on the ready-made cord.

SPIRAL
PATTERNS

SPIRAL CUSHION

*Spiral patterns have been used as symbol and
ornament throughout the span of Celtic art, from
early renderings on stone and metal, through to
elaborate designs in Christian manuscripts.
I based my Spiral Cushion on a detail from an
illuminated page in the Lindisfarne Gospels.
The sheer energy of the Lindisfarne image –
suggesting the motion and fluidity of a sea wave –
appealed to me instantly. I felt compelled to use
wool yarns in bright, contrasting colours to further
enhance the exuberant quality of the design.*

SPIRAL CUSHION

SIZE OF NEEDLEPOINT

The finished cushion/pillow measures 37cm/14½in by 38cm/15in.

MATERIALS

10-mesh single-thread canvas 51cm/20in square

Size 18 tapestry needle

Fabric for backing (and if desired, for piping/cording) and matching sewing thread

1.7m/1¾yd of ready-made cord or piping/filling cord (optional)

34cm/14in zipper

Cushion pad/pillow form 38cm/15in square

✤

APPLETON Crewel Wool (or PATERNA/YAN Persian yarn) in the following 15 colours:

A = mid green-blue
Ap 158 (or Pa 531) 182m/200yd

B = dark green-blue
Ap 159 (or Pa 530) 182m/200yd

C = pale turquoise
Ap 523 (or Pa 523) 91m/100yd

D = light turquoise
Ap 524 (or Pa 522) 22m/24yd

E = mid turquoise
Ap 525 (or Pa 574) 22m/24yd

F = deep turquoise
Ap 526 (or Pa 521) 91m/100yd

G = light yellow
Ap 693 (or Pa 733) 91m/100yd

H = yellow
Ap 694 (or Pa 742) 91m/100yd

I = autumn yellow
Ap 474 (or Pa 701) 91m/100yd

J = paprika
Ap 723 (or Pa 870) 22m/24yd

K = deep scarlet
Ap 504 (or Pa 840) 91m/100yd

L = scarlet
Ap 503 (or Pa 950) 91m/100yd

M = deep coral
Ap 866 (or Pa 850) 91m/100yd

N = coral
Ap 865 (or Pa 851) 91m/100yd

O = dusky red
Ap 206 (or Pa 872) 22m/24yd

✤

Note: For another alternative yarn brand see *Yarn Alternatives Table* on page 126. Hank and skein sizes are also given on page 126.

COLOUR MIXTURES

The embroidery for this design is worked using three strands of Appleton crewel yarn (or three strands of Paterna/yan Persian yarn). To achieve subtle shading the colours are used in combination. The colour key gives the colour combinations: for example, AAB means two strands of mid green-blue and one strand of dark green-blue used together, CCD means two strands of pale turquoise and one strand of light turquoise used together, and so on.

WORKING THE EMBROIDERY

The design covers an area 145 stitches wide by 149 stitches tall. Mark the outline of the design (and the grid lines of the chart) onto the canvas, allowing for 6.5cm/2½in of unworked canvas all around the design. If desired, stretch the canvas onto an embroidery frame. (The technical chapter beginning on page 114 gives detailed instructions for marking the canvas, stitching and finishing your needlepoint.)

Using three strands of Appleton crewel yarn (or three strands of Paterna/yan Persian yarn) in the combinations given in the colour key, work the cushion/pillow design in tent stitch following the chart on pages 40 and 41 and shading as explained below.

Shading

Although the chart shows exactly how the needlepoint has been shaded, it is not necessary to follow the chart square for square for the shading as long as the shades are sprinkled together in the same manner (see page 123). Work the entire embroidery before filling in the background. Fill in the background by working AAB and BBA at random in the remaining areas.

BLOCKING AND FINISHING

When the embroidery has been completed, block the canvas as instructed on page 124. Be sure to allow the needlepoint to dry completely before removing it from the blocking board.

Trim the unworked canvas to about 2cm/¾ in all around the edge of the needlepoint.

Backing the cushion

Using the blocked needlepoint as your template, cut two pieces of backing fabric each half the size of the trimmed canvas and with an extra seam allowance of 2cm/¾ in at the centre edge.

Insert the zipper between the two pieces of backing fabric as instructed on page 125.

To make the piping/cording, cut bias strips from the remaining backing fabric and cover the piping/filling cord. Then complete the backing for the cushion/pillow as instructed on page 125.

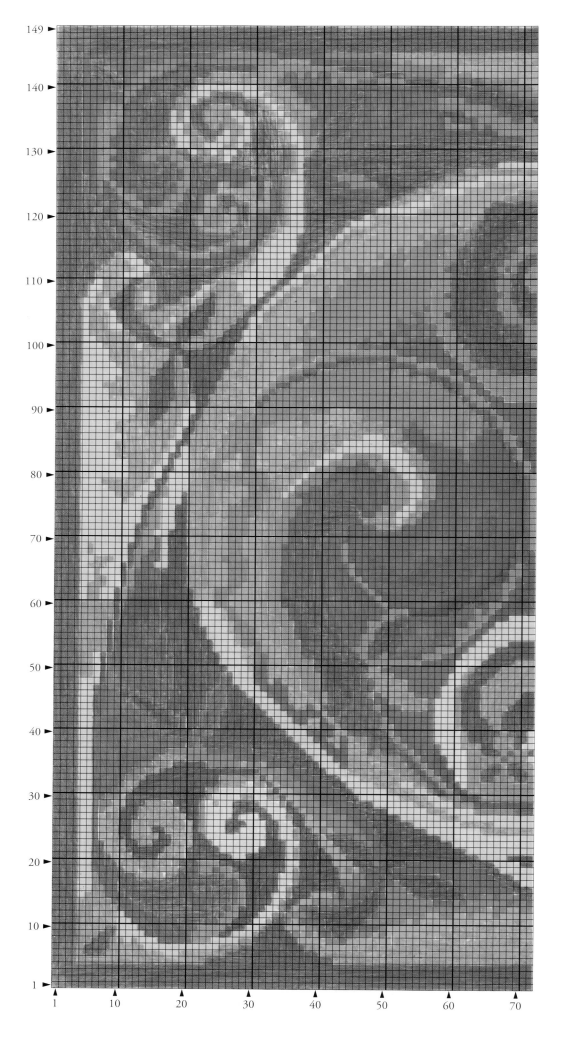

80   90   100   110   120   130   140 145

AAB and BBA

CCD

FFE

GGH

IIH

JJK

LLK

MML

NNM

OON

SPIRAL CHESSBOARD

*Some of the choicest examples of Celtic art –
rich in materials, workmanship and imagery – were
created for the aggrandisement of chieftains and
kings. I created my Spiral Chessboard in exactly
that spirit. It encompasses all the different design
elements of Celtic art. A dazzling key pattern
serves as the playing area, and the borders include
formal spirals, knotwork corners and zoomorphic
finials. The colours are suitably regal, with shades
of purples, reds and golds. This is an elaborate
design which requires time and patience in its
execution. Whether used for playing chess, or as a
wall hanging, the result is an impressive heirloom.*

SPIRAL
CHESSBOARD

SIZE OF NEEDLEPOINT

The finished needlepoint chessboard measures 62cm/24¼ in square.

MATERIALS

14-mesh single-thread canvas 76cm/29½ in square

❖

Size 20 tapestry needle

❖

Fabric for backing and matching sewing thread

❖

2.8m/3yd of ready-made decorative cord

❖

Four tassels (optional)

❖

APPLETON Crewel Wool *(or* PATERNA/YAN *Persian Yarn) in the following 16 colours:*

A = mid autumn yellow
Ap 474 (or Pa 701) 273m/300yd

B = dark autumn yellow
Ap 475 (or Pa 700) 91m/100yd

C = light gold
Ap 694 (or Pa 742) 182m/200yd

D = mid gold
Ap 695 (or Pa 732) 182m/200yd

E = paprika
Ap 723 (or Pa 870) 91m/100yd

F = scarlet
Ap 504 (or Pa 968) 273m/300yd

G = dark rose pink
Ap 225 (or Pa 930) 273m/300yd

H = mid rose pink
Ap 224 (or Pa 931) 182m/200yd

I = mauve
Ap 604 (or Pa 322) 182m/200yd

J = light purple
Ap 103 (or Pa 312) 182m/200yd

K = mid purple
Ap 104 (or Pa 311) 182m/200yd

L = dark purple
Ap 105 (or Pa 310) 182m/200yd

M = deep purple-navy
Ap 106 (or Pa 570) 22m/24yd

N = dark marine-blue
Ap 328 (or Pa 530) 22m/24yd

O = white
Ap 991 (or Pa 261) 364m/400yd

P = black
Ap 993 (or Pa 220) 364m/400yd

❖

Note: For yarn buying information see page 126. Hank and skein sizes are also given on page 126.

COLOUR MIXTURES

The embroidery for this design is worked using two strands of Appleton crewel yarn (or two strands of Paterna/yan Persian yarn). To achieve subtle shading the colours are used singly or in combination. The colour key gives the colour combinations: for example, AB means one strand of mid autumn yellow and one strand of dark autumn yellow used together, FF means two strands of scarlet used together, and so on.

WORKING THE EMBROIDERY

The design covers an area 340 stitches wide by 340 stitches tall. (The chart shows only one quarter of the chessboard.) Mark the outline of the upper left-hand corner of the design (and the grid lines of the chart) onto the canvas, allowing for 6.5cm/2½ in of unworked canvas all around the design. If desired, stretch the canvas onto an embroidery frame. (The technical chapter beginning on page 114 gives detailed instructions for marking the canvas, stitching and finishing your needlepoint.)

Using two strands of Appleton crewel yarn (or two strands of Paterna/yan Persian yarn) in the combinations given in the colour key, work the design in tent stitch. Begin by filling in the upper left-hand corner of the needlepoint, following the chart and positioning the various shades as explained below.

Shading

The squares of the chessboard are worked entirely in white (colour OO) and black (colour PP). The golds, reds and purples on the chessboard are worked in various shades and combinations of shades. The following is a guide for where to use the various shades:

Gold areas: Use random streaks of AA and AB to outline the outer border, the black and white board and the finial heads, and to work the corner knotwork panels. Use CC for the finial faces. Work the outer border "curly" pattern with alternating streaks of DD and CC. Use random streaks of AA, DD and CC for the spiral panel background.

Red areas: Use random streaks of EF and FG on the outer border background. Work the corner knotwork panel background with random streaks of GH and FG. Use random streaks of GG and EF for the red inside the spiral panels. Work the finial eyes with FF.

Light purple areas: For the background for the "curly" pattern on the outer border, use IJ only. Use random streaks of II and JJ for purple inside the spiral panels.

Darker purple areas: Use random streaks of KK and LL on the inner border background and the lower part of the finial heads.

Rotating the chart

When you have completed the design in the upper left-hand corner, turn the chart 90 degrees clockwise, so that the right edge of the chart is at the bottom. With the chart in this position, it now represents the border pattern for the upper right-hand corner of the chessboard. For the remaining two corners of the border pattern, continue rotating the chart in the same way. For the black and white board at the centre, do not follow the chart once it has been rotated, but instead continue to alternate the black and white squares by repeating the pattern set when working the upper left-hand corner of the needlepoint.

BLOCKING AND FINISHING

When the embroidery has been completed, block the canvas as instructed on page 124. Be sure to allow the needlepoint to dry completely before removing it from the blocking board.

Trim the unworked canvas to about 2cm/ ¾ in all around the edge of the needlepoint.

Backing the chessboard

Cut a piece of backing fabric the same size as the trimmed canvas.

Turn under the unworked canvas edge all around the embroidery and the same amount all around the edge of the backing fabric. Pin the backing fabric to the wrong side of the needlepoint and sew in place.

Sew the cord to the edge of the chessboard. Then sew one tassel to each corner.

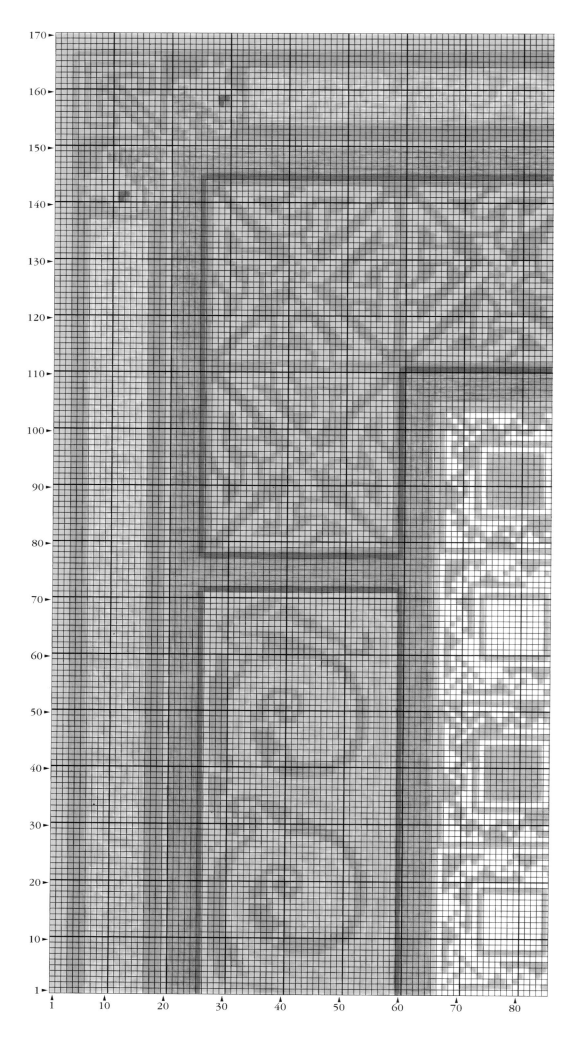

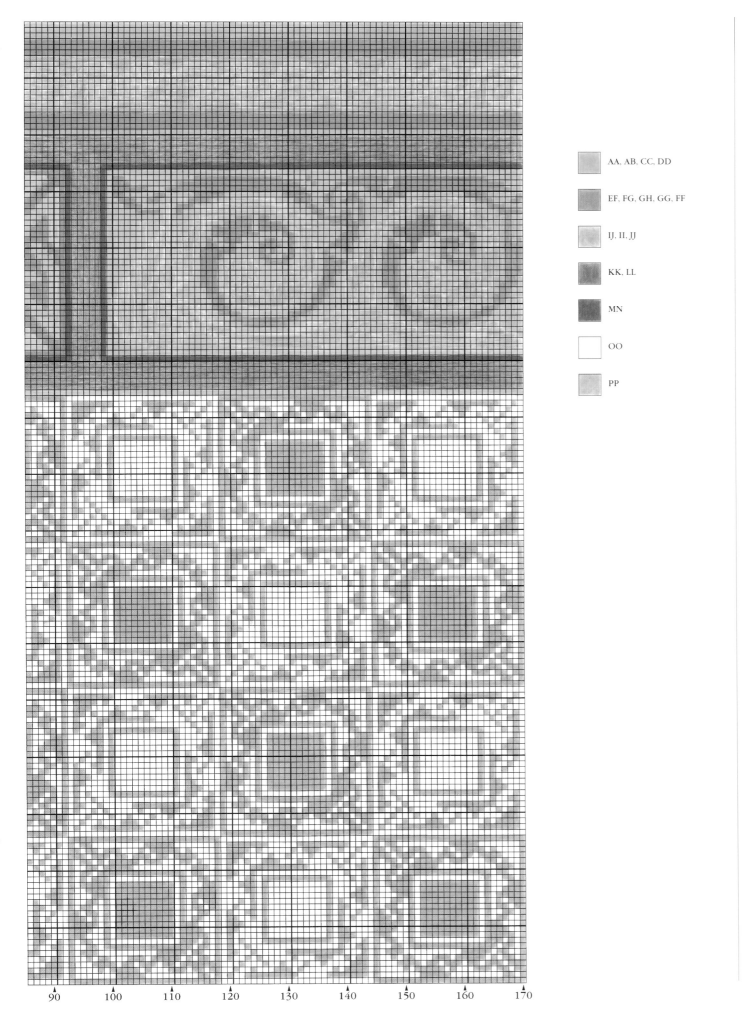

SPIRAL
SEWING CASE

*S-scroll spirals with identical centres are known
as labrys designs, and are found on some of the
very earliest Celtic artefacts. They were often used
on small metalwork objects, such as decorations for
horses bridles. The size and simplicity of these
S-scroll designs make them ideal for use in small
needlework pieces such as this sewing case.
The soft, pastel background emphasises the strong
turquoise and mauve shades of the scrolls.*

SPIRAL
SEWING CASE

SIZE OF NEEDLEPOINT

The finished spiral sewing case measures 7cm/3in by 16.5cm/3¼in when folded in half.

MATERIALS

14-mesh single-thread canvas 28cm/11¼in by 30cm/11½in

❖

Size 20 tapestry needle

❖

Fabric for lining and matching sewing thread

❖

85cm/33in of ready-made decorative cord

❖

APPLETON Crewel Wool (or PATERNA/YAN Persian Yarn) in the following 9 colours:

A = light turquoise
Ap 524 (or Pa 523) 1 skein

B = mid turquoise
Ap 525 (or Pa 522) 1 skein

C = dark turquoise
Ap 526 (or Pa 521) 1 skein

D = dark purple
Ap 455 (or Pa 311) 1 skein

E = mid purple
Ap 453 (or Pa 300) 1 skein

F = pale lilac
Ap 884 (or Pa 314) 1 skein

G= pale pink
Ap 141 (or Pa 924) 1 skein

H = mid mauve
Ap 604 (or Pa 322) 1 skein

I = pale mauve
Ap 601 (or Pa 324) 1 skein

❖

Note: The alternative yarn brand (in parentheses) will not give *exactly* the same effect as the original brand, as colours will never match exactly from yarn brand to yarn brand. See yarn buying information on page 126 and suppliers addresses on page 127.

COLOUR MIXTURES

The embroidery for the *Spiral Sewing Case* is worked using two strands of Appleton crewel yarn (or two strands of Paterna/yan Persian yarn). To achieve subtle shading the colours are used singly or they are used in combination.

The colour key gives the colour combinations: for example, AB means one strand of light turquoise and one strand of mid turquoise used together, DD means two strands of dark purple used together, HH means two strands of mid mauve used together, and so on. (See pages 52 and 53 for the chart for this design.)

WORKING THE EMBROIDERY

The design covers an area 91 stitches wide by 87 stitches tall. Mark the outline of the entire design (and the grid lines of the chart) onto the canvas, allowing for 6.5cm/2½in of unworked canvas all around the design. If desired, stretch the canvas onto an embroidery frame. (The technical chapter beginning on page 114 gives detailed instructions for marking the canvas, stitching and finishing your needlepoint.)

Using two strands of Appleton crewel yarn (or two strands of Paterna/yan Persian yarn) in the combinations given in the colour key, work the design in tent stitch. Leaving the background until last, begin by working the border and the spiral pattern, shading as explained below.

Shading the border and leaves

First, fill in the outer border and the "leaves" with random streaks of EE and HH.

Shading the spiral pattern

For the dark purple "centres" of the spirals use DD and shade gradually through EE to HH at the end of the spiral. For the dark turquoise around the centre "leaf" use CC and shade gradually from here towards each end through BC, BB and AB to AA at the centre of each spiral.

Shading the background

Fill in the remaining pastel background with random streaks of shades FG and FI.

BLOCKING AND FINISHING

When the embroidery has been completed, block the canvas as instructed on page 124. Be sure to allow the needlepoint to dry completely before removing it from the blocking board.

Trim the unworked canvas to about 2cm/ ¾ in all around the edge of the needlepoint.

Lining the sewing case

Cut a piece of lining the same size as the trimmed canvas. Before attaching the lining, make any desired additions, such as a small loop to hold your scissors or small hemmed flaps for pins and needles, etc.

Then place the lining on top of the needlepoint with the right sides together and pin. Sew the lining in place, using backstitch or using a sewing machine with a zipper foot. Work the stitches close to the embroidery and leave one side open for turning.

Clip the seam allowance diagonally at the two corners. Then turn the sewing case inside out.

Close the opening with small slipstitches, leaving the last 1cm/ ¼ in unworked.

Sew the cord to the sewing case along the seamline, beginning at the small opening and tucking the ends into the inside. Close the small opening with slipstitches, securing the ends of the cord in the process.

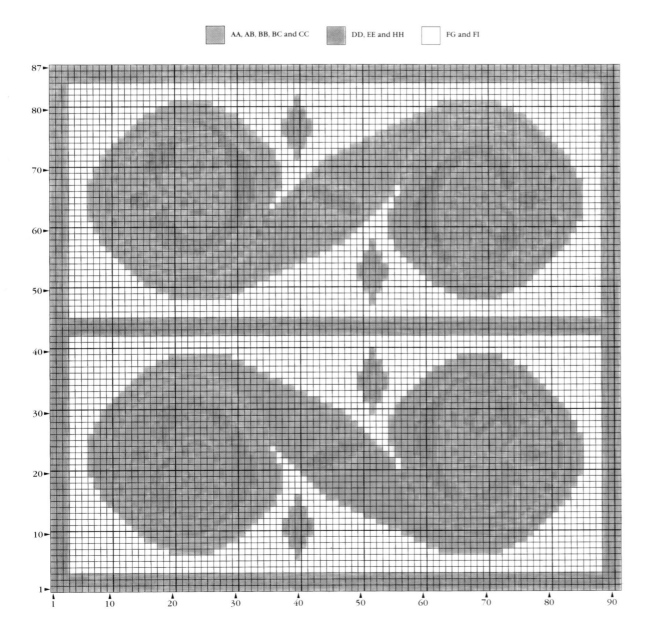

SPIRAL
PINCUSHION

*The beautiful little pattern on the
Spiral Pincushion could be equally described as a
spiral knotwork or a knotwork spiral, for it is a
combination of both. I found it as a small detail on
a very elaborate page of the Book of Kells.
This composition serves as an example of how such
details can often be abstracted from the page to
stand alone with perfect poise. The pincushion is a
quick project to make, and is therefore an ideal
starting point for a newcomer to the concepts of
Celtic design.*

SPIRAL PINCUSHION

SIZE OF NEEDLEPOINT

The finished needlepoint pincushion measures 9cm/3½in square.

MATERIALS

14-mesh single-thread canvas 22cm/8½in square

❖

Size 20 tapestry needle

❖

Fabric for backing and matching sewing thread

❖

45cm/½yd of ready-made decorative cord

❖

Four 5cm/2in-long tassels

❖

Small amount of polyester filling/stuffing

❖

APPLETON Crewel Wool (or PATERNA/YAN Persian Yarn) in the following 5 colours:

A = autumn yellow
Ap 474 (or Pa 732) 1 skein

B = gold
Ap 695 (or Pa 733) 1 skein

C = mid marine blue
Ap 325 (or Pa 511) 1 skein

D = dark marine blue
Ap 327 (or Pa 510) 1 skein

E = deepest marine blue
Ap 328 (or Pa 530) 1 skein

❖

Note: The alternative yarn brand (in parentheses) will not give *exactly* the same effect as the original brand, as colours will never match exactly from yarn brand to yarn brand.

COLOUR MIXTURES

The embroidery for this design is worked using two strands of Appleton crewel yarn (or two strands of Paterna/yan Persian yarn). To achieve subtle shading the colours are used in combination. The colour key gives the colour combinations: AB means one strand of autumn yellow and one strand of gold used together, CD means one strand of mid marine blue and one strand of dark marine blue used together, and DE means one strand of dark marine blue and one strand of deepest marine blue used together.

WORKING THE EMBROIDERY

The design covers an area 51 stitches wide by 51 stitches tall. Mark the outline of the entire design (and the grid lines of the chart) onto the canvas, allowing for 6.5cm/2½in of unworked canvas all around the pincushion design.

If desired, stretch the canvas onto an embroidery frame. (The technical chapter beginning on page 114 gives detailed instructions for marking the canvas, stitching and finishing your needlepoint.)

Using two strands of Appleton crewel yarn (or two strands of Paterna/yan Persian yarn) in the combinations given in the colour key, work the design in tent stitch. Leaving the background until last, begin by working the spiral pattern on the needlepoint, shading as explained below.

Shading the spiral pattern

The spiral pattern on the needlepoint is worked with one shade only – AB.

Shading the background

After completing the spiral pattern, work the background in random streaks of CD and DE.

BLOCKING AND FINISHING

When the embroidery has been completed, block the canvas as instructed on page 124. Be sure to allow the needlepoint to dry completely before removing it from the blocking board.

Trim the unworked canvas to about 2cm/¾in all around the edge of the needlepoint.

Choosing the backing fabric

The backing fabric for the bookmark should match as closely as possible one of the colours in the needlepoint. It should be of a medium weight, in keeping with the weight of the needlepoint.

Backing the pincushion

Press the backing fabric before cutting. Then cut a piece of backing fabric the same size as the trimmed needlepoint canvas.

Place the backing on top of the needlepoint with the right sides together and pin. Sew the backing in place, using backstitch or using a sewing machine with a zipper foot. Work the stitches close to the embroidery and leave one side open for turning and stuffing.

Clip the seam allowance diagonally at the two corners. Then turn the pincushion right side out.

Stuff the pincushion firmly. Close the opening with small slipstitches, leaving the last 1cm/¼in unworked.

Sew the cord to the pincushion along the seamline, beginning at the small opening and tucking the ends into the inside of the pincushion. Close the small opening with slipstitches, securing the ends in the process. Sew one tassel to each corner.

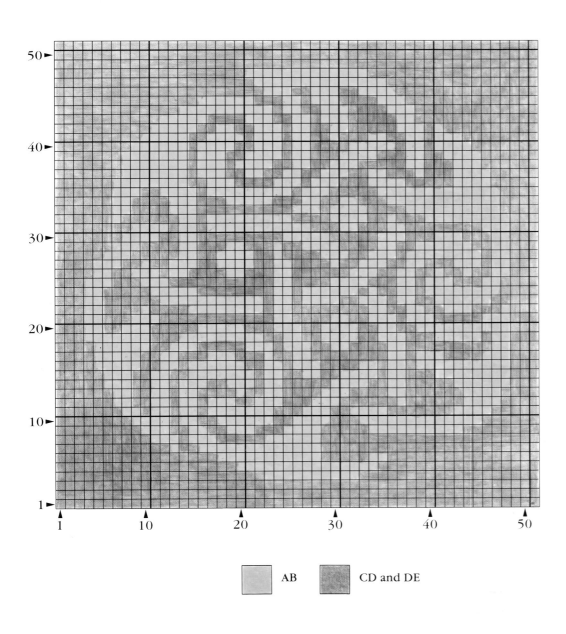

AB   CD and DE

KNOTWORK
PATTERNS

HEXAGONAL KNOTWORK CUSHION

Interlacing knotwork is the most universally known type of Celtic pattern, although it actually appeared at a later stage in Celtic art than spiral and key patterns. Knotwork is particularly associated with the Pictish stonework of eastern Scotland. The unbroken line – as a symbol of continuity – has a special power for me, and never more so than when it is worked in stone.
For my Hexagonal Knotwork Cushion I chose dark, moody colours to suggest the antiquity of stonework, and to add strength to the two continuous, interlaced lines which form the hexagonal design.

HEXAGONAL KNOTWORK CUSHION

SIZE OF NEEDLEPOINT

The finished cushion/pillow measures 44cm/17¼ in across the centre between two points of the hexagonal shape.

MATERIALS

10-mesh single-thread canvas 53cm/20¾ in by 57cm/22½ in

❖

Size 18 tapestry needle

❖

Fabric for backing (and if desired, for piping/cording) and matching sewing thread

❖

1.9m/2yd of ready-made cord or piping/filling cord (optional)

❖

38cm/15in zipper

❖

Hexagon cushion pad/pillow form to fit finished cover

❖

APPLETON Tapestry Wool (or DMC Laine Colbert tapestry yarn) in the following 4 colours:

A = dark marine blue
Ap 327 (or DMC 7288) 165m/180yd

B = dark green-blue
Ap 159 (or DMC 7999) 55m/60yd

C = iron grey
Ap 964 (or DMC 7273) 110m/120yd

D = light dull mauve
Ap 931 (or DMC 7234) 83m/90yd

❖

Note: For alternative yarn brands see *Yarn Alternatives Table* on page 127. Hank and skein sizes are given on page 126.

ALTERNATIVE COLOURWAYS

Because this design is so simple, it is the ideal project on which to try your own individual colour theme.

When changing a colourway to suit your own tastes, it is best to test how the colours work before purchasing the entire amount of yarn required. With just a small skein of each of the four colours, you can stitch up a tiny area where all four colours meet. Colours will always look slightly different when they are stitched next to other colours, than they look when skeins are simply held next to each other.

WORKING THE EMBROIDERY

The design covers an area 173 stitches across the centre and 156 stitches from top to bottom. (The chart shows only half of the design.) Mark the outline of the design (and the grid lines of the chart) onto the canvas, allowing for 6.5cm/2½ in of unworked canvas all around the design. If desired, stretch the canvas onto an embroidery frame. (The technical chapter beginning on page 114 gives detailed instructions for marking the canvas, stitching and finishing.)

Using one strand of Appleton tapestry yarn (or one strand of DMC Laine Colbert), work the outlines of the knotwork patterns on the bottom half of the design in tent stitch, using colour B (dark green-blue) and following the chart. Then complete the knotwork patterns on the bottom half of the design by filling in with colours C (iron grey) and D (light dull mauve) as shown on the chart.

Rotating the chart

When you have completed the bottom half of the design (through row 78) with the exception of the background, turn the chart upside down and follow the upside-down chart for the top half of the knotwork patterns, but omitting the centre row of stitches (row 78) and leaving the background until last.

Filling in the background

Once you have completed the knotwork patterns, fill in the background using colour A (dark marine blue) as indicated on the chart.

Due to the simplicity of this needlepoint design, the background could be worked in basketweave tent stitch. This stitch tends to distort the canvas much less than either continental stitch or the half cross technique. See pages 119 and 120 for the various methods used for forming tent stitches.

MAKING A RECTANGULAR CUSHION

To make a rectangular cushion, fill in the corners of the design by extending the background, using colour A (dark marine blue).

BLOCKING AND FINISHING

When the embroidery has been completed, block the canvas as instructed on page 124. Be sure to allow the needlepoint to dry completely before removing it from the blocking board.

Trim the unworked canvas to about 2cm/¾ in all around the edge of the needlepoint.

Backing the cushion

Using the blocked needlepoint as your template, cut two pieces of backing fabric each half the size of the trimmed canvas and with an extra seam allowance of 2cm/¾ in at the centre. (The centre seam of the backing should run perpendicular to the base of the design as it appears on the chart.)

Insert the zipper between the two pieces of backing fabric as instructed on page 125.

To make the piping/cording, cut bias strips from the remaining backing fabric and cover the piping/filling cord. Complete the backing as instructed on page 125.

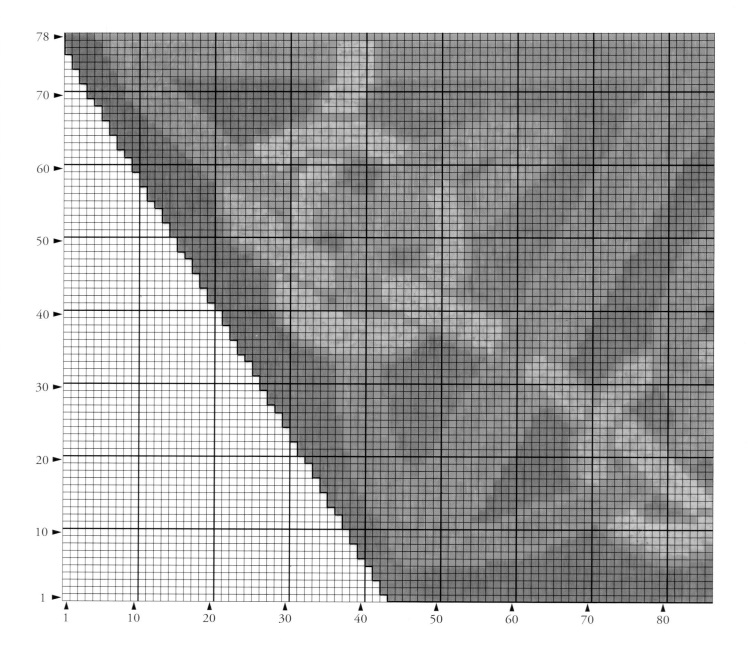

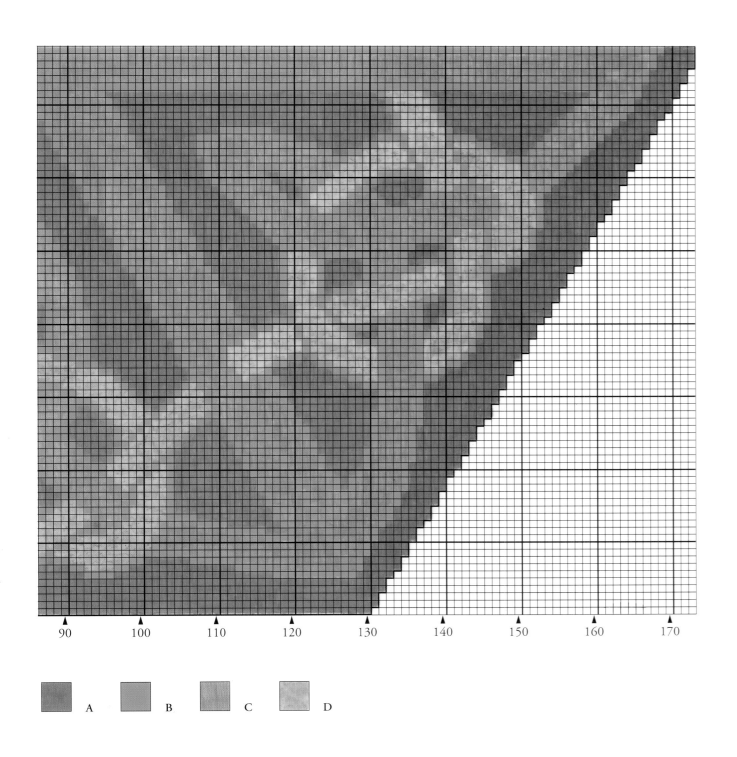

90   100   110   120   130   140   150   160   170

A   B   C   D

KNOTWORK
BELT

*Interlacing patterns have often been used in
Celtic design as borders or frames for larger
designs. It was this linear quality that suggested
that they could be ideally used in a belt.
I chose a regular and repeating pattern for my
Knotwork Belt so that it could be made in any
length. Because I wanted the pattern to dominate,
I selected suitably muted colours. But it would be
very easy for you to substitute your own colours
for a completely different effect.*

KNOTWORK
BELT

SIZE OF NEEDLEPOINT

The finished belt measures 5cm/2in wide by the desired length.

Note: The belt pictured measures approximately 62cm/24½in long. The recommended yarn amounts, however, are generous and are enough for up to a 112cm/44in belt.

MATERIALS

18-mesh single-thread canvas 18cm/7in wide by the desired finished belt length plus 17cm/6½in extra

Size 22 tapestry needle

Small amount of fabric for belt backing and matching sewing thread

Belt buckle in two parts

APPLETON Crewel Wool (or PATERNA/YAN Persian Yarn) in the following 3 colours:

A = black
Ap 993 (or Pa 220) 273m/300yd

B = dark iron grey
Ap 964 (or Pa 202) 182m/200yd

C = light iron grey
Ap 962 (or Pa 203) 182m/200yd

Note: For another alternative yarn brand see *Yarn Alternatives Table* on page 127. Hank and skein sizes are given on page 126.

CALCULATING BELT LENGTH

In order to calculate how long to work the needlepoint belt, first decide on the finished length you will need in order to encompass the waist comfortably.

From the desired finished belt length subtract the length of the belt buckle. To this result, add 4cm/1½in so that there is an allowance for a turn back of 2cm/¾in at each end of the belt. This will give you the total length required for the needlepoint.

WORKING THE EMBROIDERY

The design covers an area 38 stitches tall by the desired length (see above for calculating length).

Mark the outline of the design (and the grid line of the chart) onto the canvas, allowing for 6.5cm/2½in of unworked canvas all around the design. If desired, stretch the canvas onto an embroidery frame. (The technical chapter beginning on page 114 gives detailed instructions for marking the canvas, stitching and finishing your needlepoint.)

Using two strands of Appleton crewel yarn (or one strand of Paterna/yan Persian yarn), work the design in tent stitch following the chart.

Begin by working the left-hand end of the belt and the first 20-stitch knotwork pattern repeat. Then repeat the 20-stitch pattern repeat until the belt measures 3cm/1½in shorter than the desired finished length and complete the belt by working the right-hand end.

BLOCKING AND FINISHING

When the embroidery has been completed, block the canvas as instructed on page 124. Be sure to allow the needlepoint to dry completely before removing it from the blocking board.

Trim the unworked canvas to about 1.5cm/½in all around the edge of the needlepoint.

Choosing the backing fabric

The backing fabric for the bookmark should match as closely as possible one of the colours in the needlepoint. It should be of a fine weight, in keeping with the needlepoint.

Backing the belt

Press the fabric gently before cutting. Then cut a piece of backing fabric the same size as the trimmed canvas. Turn under the unworked canvas edge all around the embroidery and pin in this position, with the pins perpendicular to the edge so that they can be easily removed once the lining is in place.

Turn the seam allowance on the piece of backing fabric to the wrong side and tack/baste it in position, using a contrasting sewing thread. Press the backing.

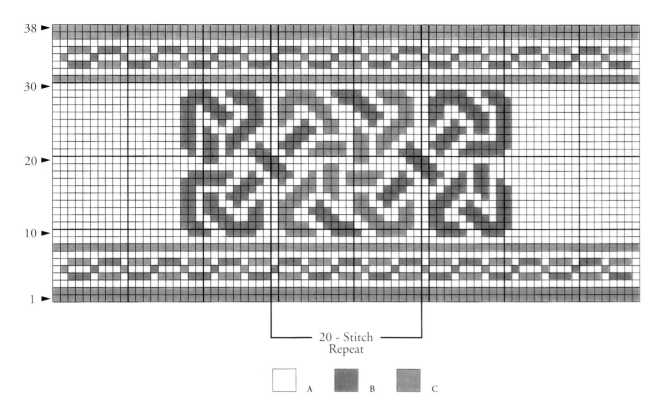

38 ►
30 ►
20 ►
10 ►
1 ►

20 - Stitch
Repeat

A   B   C

Then pin the backing fabric to the belt with the wrong sides together. Using the matching sewing thread and a sewing needle, sew the backing to the needlepoint with small, even slipstitches. Remove the pins and the tacking/basting thread.

Slip one end of the belt into one part of the buckle, fold under the first fourteen rows of stitches and sew to the wrong side of the belt.

Attach the other part of the buckle to the opposite end in the same way.

KNOTWORK
CARPET SEAT
CUSHION

The term "carpet" is applied to Celtic designs where patterns are inlaid within other patterns, simply because of their resemblance to Persian rugs. This is not to suggest that there is any connection between the these two distinct streams of decorative art. The Knotwork Carpet Cushion contains four bold knotwork insets, which contrast with the finer tracery of the surrounding interlacings and spiral patterns. Although the individual pattern elements are simple, the arrangement creates an elaborate and regal appearance.

68

KNOTWORK CARPET
SEAT CUSHION

SIZE OF NEEDLEPOINT

The finished cushion measures 40cm/15½in square by 4cm/1½in deep.

MATERIALS

10-mesh single-thread canvas 61cm/24in square

Size 18 tapestry needle

Fabric for backing and matching sewing thread

Foam rubber cushion pad/pillow form cut to fit finished needlepoint

APPLETON Crewel Wool (or PATERNA/YAN Persian Yarn) in the following 6 colours:

A = scarlet
Ap 503 (or Pa 950) 364m/400yd

B = deep scarlet
Ap 504 (or Pa 968) 364m/400yd

C = deep coral
Ap 866 (or Pa 850) 364m/400yd

D = light brown-olive
Ap 311 (or Pa 752) 182m/200yd

E = autumn yellow
Ap 474 (or Pa 701) 182m/200yd

F = gold
Ap 695 (or Pa 732) 182m/200yd

Note: For another alternative yarn brand see *Yarn Alternatives Table* on page 127. Hank and skein sizes are given on page 126.

COLOUR MIXTURES

The embroidery for this design is worked using three strands of Appleton crewel yarn (or three strands of Paterna/yan Persian yarn). To achieve subtle shading the colours are used singly or in combination. The colour key gives the colour combinations: for example, DDE means two strands of mid light brown-olive and one strand of autumn yellow used together, BBB means three strands of deep scarlet used together, FFF means three strands of gold used together, and so on.

WORKING THE EMBROIDERY

The design covers an area 189 stitches wide by 189 stitches tall. Mark the outline of the design onto the canvas, allowing for 6.5cm/2½in of unworked canvas all around the design. If desired, stretch the canvas onto an embroidery frame. (The technical chapter beginning on page 114 gives detailed instructions for marking the canvas, stitching and finishing.)

Using three strands of Appleton crewel yarn (or three strands of Paterna/yan Persian yarn) in the combinations given in the colour key, work the design in tent stitch. Leaving the background until last, begin by working the gold patterns, following the chart and shading as explained below.

Shading the patterns

The gold patterns on the needlepoint are worked with nine shades created by mixing yarns D, E and F. When embroidering the gold patterns, work random streaks of DDD, EEE, FFF, DDE, DDF, EED, EEF, FFD and FFE.

Shading the background

Fill in the background with random streaks of only three shades – AAA, BBB and CCC.

BLOCKING AND FINISHING

When the embroidery has been completed, block the canvas as instructed on page 124. Be sure to allow the needlepoint to dry completely before removing it from the blocking board.

Cushion pad/pillow form

After the needlepoint has been blocked, measure the depth of the sides that will be turned down to form the squared corners. Then measure the width of the "top" of the cushion between the sides to be turned down. Measure this width in both directions.

Take these measurements to a shop that will cut foam rubber pieces to any size.

Seaming the corners

Trim the unworked canvas to about 2cm/ ¾ in all around the edge of the needlepoint.

Fold the sides of one corner together, so that the wrong sides of the canvas are facing and the canvas holes are lined up. Using two strands of B and one strand of C and the tapestry needle, join the corner seam with tent stitch. Join the remaining three corner seams in the same way.

Backing the cushion

Insert the foam rubber cushion pad/pillow form.

Fold the unworked canvas edge to the wrong side all around the edge of the embroidery.

Then cut a piece of backing fabric the same size as the top of the cushion plus a 2cm/ ¾ in seam allowance all around the edge. Turn under the seam allowance around the edge of the fabric and press. Pin the backing to the needlepoint and sew in place.

COLOUR KEY

AAA, BBB, CCC

DDD, EEE, FFF
and other combinations
of D, E and F

BIRD AND TREE PATTERNS

EAGLE TILE
CUSHION

*The identifying symbols of the four Evangelists
are central to the imagery of the Book of Kells.
Matthew is a man; Mark is a lion; Luke is a calf,
and John is the eagle. The Eagle Tile Cushion is
a faithful copy – straight from one of the pages of
the Book of Kells – of my favourite depiction of the
eagle symbol. It is a supernatural image with a
wild, unearthly quality, both in form – note the two
pairs of wings – and in colour. This is a classic
example of the pagan Celtic culture having acquired
a Christian purpose.*

EAGLE TILE CUSHION

SIZE OF NEEDLEPOINT

The finished needlepoint cushion/pillow measures 43cm/16¾in square.

MATERIALS

10-mesh single-thread canvas 56cm/21¾in square

❖

Size 18 tapestry needle

❖

Fabric for backing (and if desired, for piping/cording) and matching sewing thread

❖

40cm/16in zipper

❖

1.9m/2yd of ready-made cord or piping cord (optional)

❖

40cm/16in zipper

❖

Cushion pad/pillow form 43cm/17in square

❖

APPLETON Tapestry Wool (or DMC Laine Colbert tapestry yarn) in the following 22 colours:

A = dull mauve
Ap 932 (or DMC 7234) 19m/20yd

B = light dull mauve
Ap 931 (or DMC 7232) 10m/11yd

C = salmon
Ap 143 (or DMC 7226) 14m/16yd

D = cinnamon
Ap 765 (or DMC 7508) 7m/8yd

E = light pink
Ap 142 (or DMC 7223) 13m/14yd

F = deep pink
Ap 146 (or DMC 7208) 27m/29yd

G = dark scarlet
Ap 505 (or DMC 7110) 26m/28yd

H = mid scarlet
Ap 504 (or DMC 7127) 23m/25yd

I = purple
Ap 104 (or DMC 7242) 13m/14yd

J = lavender
Ap 101 (or DMC 7711) 12m/13yd

K = pale lavender
Ap 884 (or DMC 7722) 9m/10yd

L = gold
Ap 843 (or DMC 7473) 17m/19yd

M = light gold
Ap 473 (or DMC 7504) 24m/26yd

N = dark blue
Ap 327 (or DMC 7288) 13m/14yd

O = mid blue
Ap 568 (or DMC 7311) 19m/20yd

P = light blue
Ap 324 (or DMC 7592) 21m/23yd

Q = light fawn
Ap 981 (or DMC 7520) 42m/46yd

R = charcoal
Ap 998 (or DMC 7624) 24m/26yd

S = pale blue
Ap 152 (or DMC 7692) 10m/11yd

T = mid green
Ap 293 (or DMC 7394) 19m/20yd

U = pale olive
Ap 241 (or DMC 7361) 19m/20yd

V = dark green
Ap 159 (or DMC 7999) 14m/16yd

❖

Note: For alternative yarn brands see *Yarn Alternatives Table* on page 127. Hank and skein sizes are given on page 126.

YARN AMOUNTS

The recommended yarn amounts are generous. They are more than enough for working the design in basketweave or continental tent stitch. If your are working the design in half cross stitch, up to 40 per cent less yarn may be needed.

In order to calculate how many skeins of a particular yarn to buy, turn to page 126 for the approximate metrage/yardage per skein. If you are working the design in half cross stitch, you will need about 30 per cent less of each colour.

Also, if the amount required of a particular colour is just over the skein length, it is wise to buy just one skein to start and buy more later only if it is needed. If the amount required is just over the length of two skeins, then buy just two skeins to start, and so on.

Alternatively, you could buy enough skeins to cover the recommended amounts and return any leftover skeins. If you are planning to do this, however, check with your yarn shop that they will accept returned skeins of needlepoint yarn.

WORKING THE EMBROIDERY

The design covers an area 168 stitches wide by 167 stitches tall. Mark the outline of the design (and the grid lines of the chart) onto the canvas, allowing for 6.5cm/2½in of unworked canvas all around the design. If desired, stretch the canvas onto an embroidery frame. (The technical chapter beginning on page 114 gives detailed instructions for marking the canvas, stitching and finishing your needlepoint.)

Using one strand of Appleton tapestry yarn (or one strand of DMC Laine Colbert), work the design in tent stitch following the chart on pages 80 and 81.

Shading

It is not necessary to follow the chart square for square in the shaded areas (such as the outer border) as long as the shades are sprinkled together in the same manner.

BLOCKING AND FINISHING

When the embroidery has been completed, block the canvas as instructed on page 124. Be sure to allow the needlepoint to dry completely before removing it from the blocking board.

Trim the unworked canvas to about 2cm/¾in all around the edge of the needlepoint.

Backing the cushion

Using the blocked needlepoint as your template, cut two pieces of backing fabric each half the size of the trimmed canvas and with an extra seam allowance of 2cm/¾in at the centre.

Insert the zipper between the two pieces of backing fabric as instructed on page 125.

To make the piping/cording, cut bias strips from the remaining backing fabric and cover the piping/filling cord. Complete the backing as instructed on page 125.

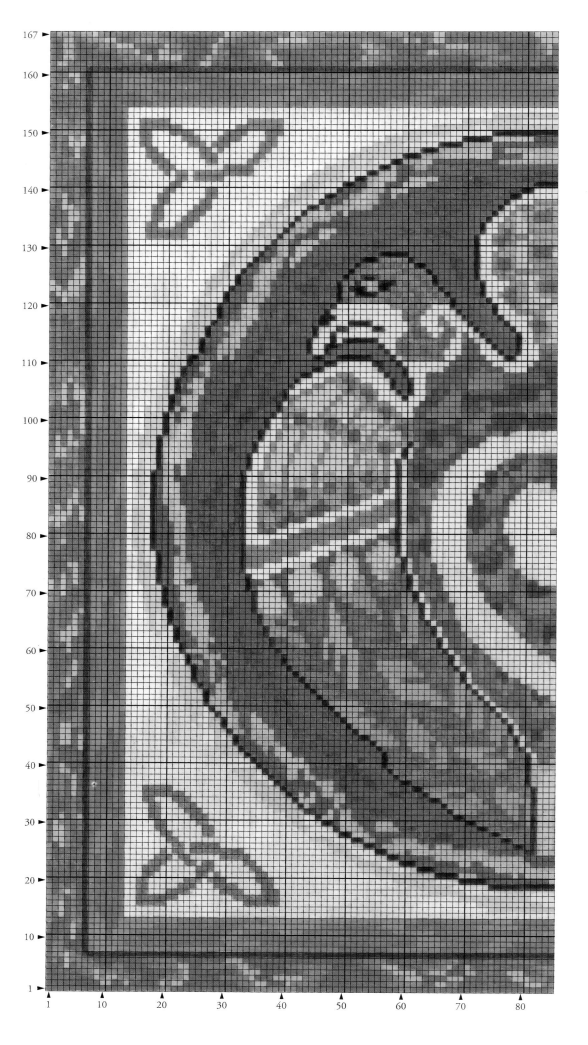

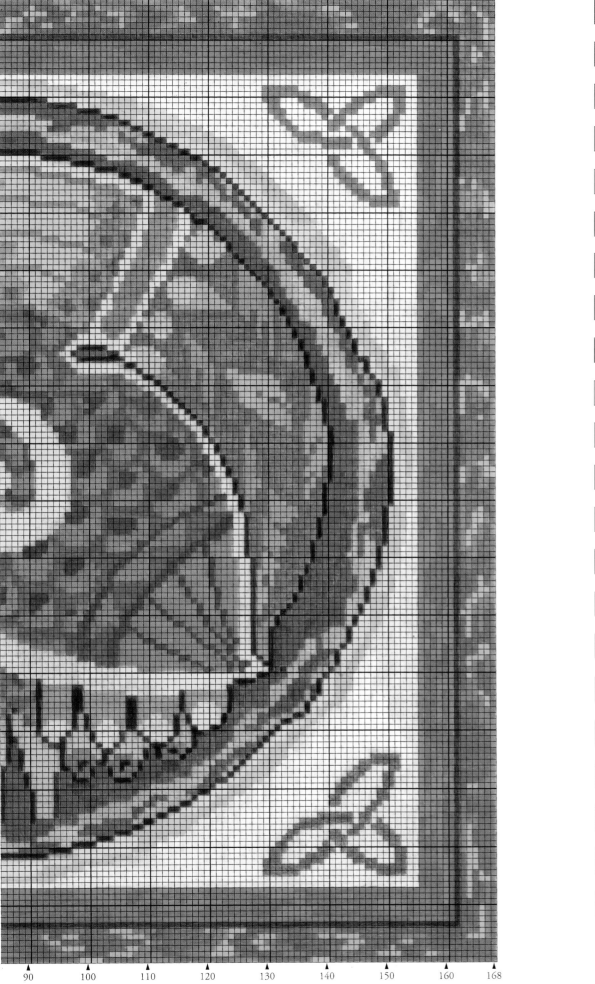

A
B
C
D
E
F
G
H
I
J
K
L
M
N
O
P
Q
R
S
T
U
V

INTERLACED
HERON
BOOKMARK

*Celtic illuminated manuscripts abound with
waterbird designs, possibly suggesting a
meaningful connection of the two elements, air and
water. In the Book of Kells waterbird forms mainly
occur as linear, interlaced designs. Here, I have
interlaced two birds with a swirling line of fine
knotwork. The Interlaced Heron Bookmark is
worked in stranded silk embroidery thread on a fine
canvas to produce an effect that is delicate
and luxurious.*

INTERLACED HERON BOOKMARK

SIZE OF NEEDLEPOINT

The finished bookmark measures 4cm/1¾in wide by 22cm/8½in long.

MATERIALS

22-mesh single-thread canvas 18cm/7in by 35cm/13½in

Size 24 tapestry needle

Small amount of fabric for bookmark backing and matching sewing thread

KREINIK *Soie d'Alger stranded silk embroidery thread/floss (or DMC Stranded Cotton embroidery thread/floss) in the following 8 colours:*

A = light gold
Kr 2212 (or DMC 3046) 1 skein

B = orange
Kr 2546 (or DMC 741) 1 skein

C = green
Kr 235 (or DMC 988) 1 skein

D = bright blue
Kr 114 (or DMC 996) 1 skein

E = dark crimson
Kr 945 (or DMC 304) 1 skein

F = scarlet
Kr 936 (or DMC 349) 1 skein

G = musk
Kr 4612 (or DMC 356) 1 skein

H = dark blue and dark green
Kr 1716 (or DMC 311) 1 skein
and Kr 206 (or DMC 500) 1 skein

Note: For another alternative yarn brand see *Yarn Alternatives Table* on page 127. The alternative brands will not give *exactly* the same effect as the silk thread/floss.

WORKING THE EMBROIDERY

The design covers an area 37 stitches wide by 188 stitches long. Mark the outline of the design (and the grid lines of the chart) onto the canvas, allowing for 6.5cm/2½in of unworked canvas all around the design. If desired, stretch the canvas onto an embroidery frame. (The technical chapter beginning on page 114 gives detailed instructions for marking the canvas, stitching and finishing your needlepoint.)

The chart for the bookmark is illustrated in two separate sections, but the design should be worked in a continuous strip. Using two strands of Soie d'Alger stranded silk embroidery thread/floss (or two strands of DMC stranded cotton embroidery thread/ floss) and leaving the background until last, work the design in tent stitch following the chart. For the background use one strand of dark blue and one strand of dark green together.

BLOCKING AND FINISHING

When the embroidery has been completed, block the canvas very gently as instructed on page 124. Be sure to allow the needlepoint to dry completely before removing it from the blocking board.

Trim the unworked canvas to about 1.5cm/ ½in all around the edge of the needlepoint.

Choosing the backing fabric

The backing fabric for the bookmark should match as closely as possible one of the colours in the needlepoint. It should be of a very fine weight, in keeping with the delicacy of the needlepoint.

If the embroidery has been worked in stranded silk embroidery thread/floss, a lightweight lining silk would be a suitable backing fabric. If it has been worked in stranded cotton embroidery thread/floss, a lightweight cotton or linen would be a good choice for the backing.

Backing the bookmark

Press the fabric gently before cutting. Then cut a piece of backing fabric the same size as the trimmed canvas.

Turn under the unworked canvas edge all around the embroidery and pin in this position, with the pins perpendicular to the edge so that they can be easily removed once the lining is in place.

Turn the seam allowance on the piece of backing fabric to the wrong side and tack/baste it in position, using a contrasting sewing thread. Press the backing.

Then pin the backing fabric to the bookmark with the wrong sides together. Using the matching sewing thread and a sewing needle, sew the backing to the needlepoint with small, even slipstitches. Remove the pins and the tacking/basting thread.

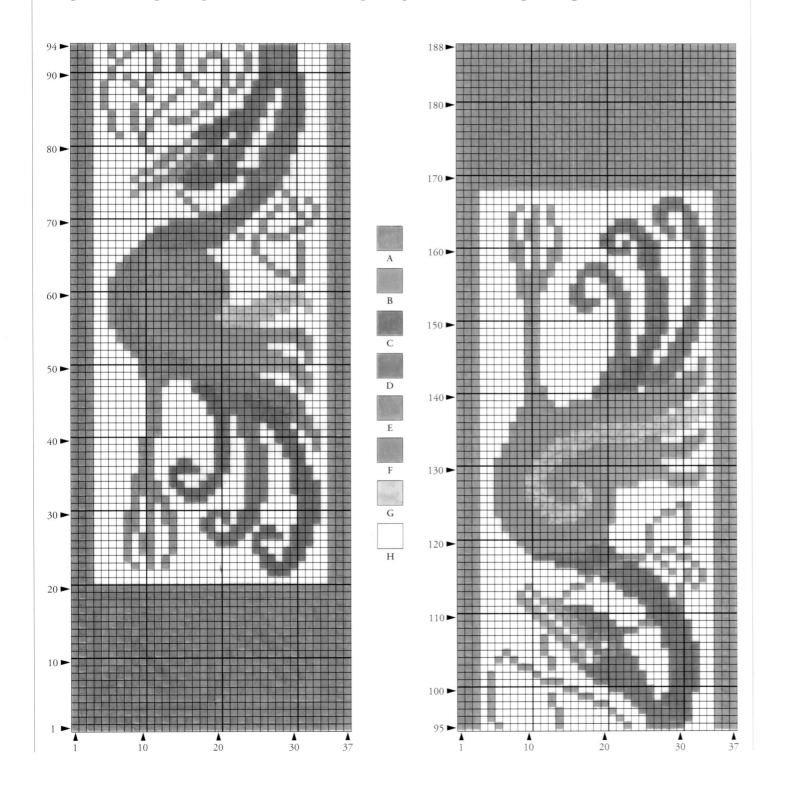

TREE OF LIFE PANEL

The use of plant imagery in Celtic art only became common in the Christian era. The tree of life, or fountain, was a metaphor central to Celtic beliefs. The tree or plant always emerges from a pot or vase, with growth coming from the main stem. Some examples are more complex than others, being packed with fruits, birds and mammals. My Tree of Life Panel is a simple and elegant version, worked in soft random shades on a mottled blue background.

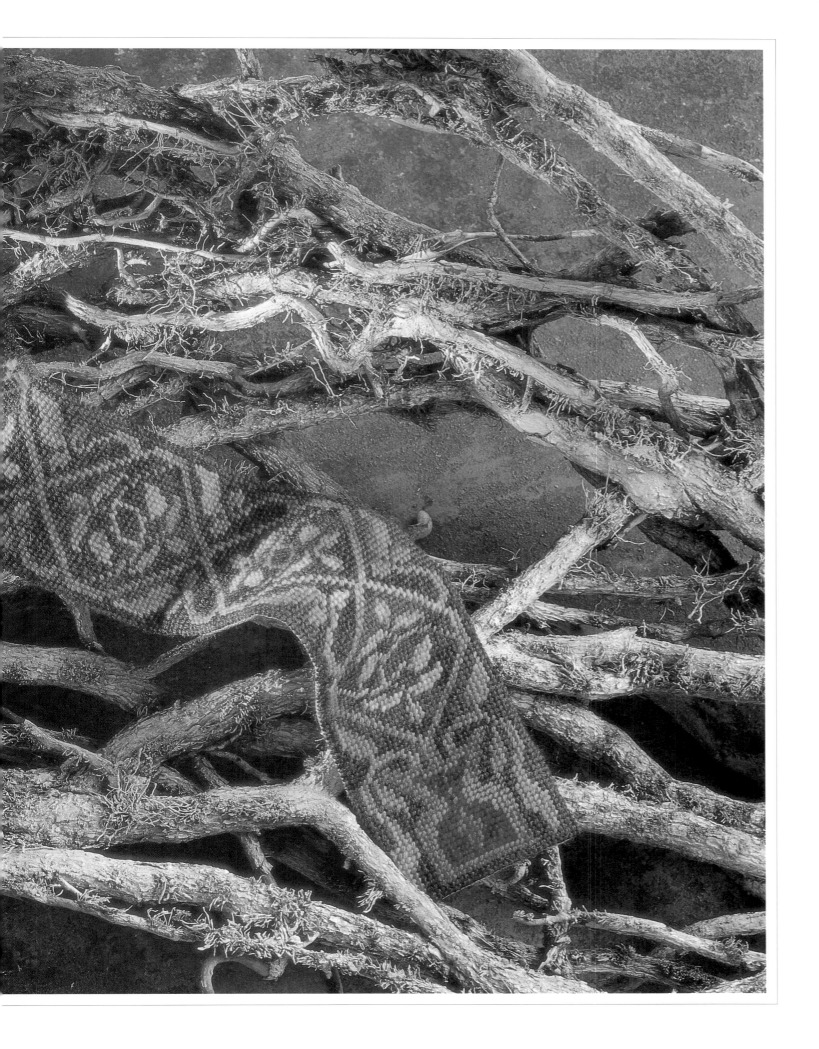

TREE OF LIFE
PANEL

SIZE OF NEEDLEPOINT

The finished needlepoint panel measures 9cm/3½in wide by 58cm/22¾in long and can be backed with fabric or framed.

MATERIALS

10-mesh single-thread canvas 51cm/8½in by 71cm/27¾in

Size 18 tapestry needle

Fabric for backing (optional) and matching sewing thread

APPLETON Tapestry Wool (or DMC Laine Colbert tapestry wool) in the following 18 colours:

A = dark blue
Ap 926 (or DMC 7306) 3 skeins

B = blue
Ap 566 (or DMC 7595) 7 skeins

C = deep pink
Ap 146 (or DMC 7208) 1 skein

D = salmon
Ap 143 (or DMC 7226) 1 skein

E = light pink
Ap 142 (or DMC 7223) 1 skein

F = pale pink
Ap141 (or DMC 7230) 1 skein

G = dusky coral
Ap 204 (or DMC 7166) 1 skein

H = bright rose pink
Ap 223 (or DMC 7217) 1 skein

I = sienna
Ap 698 (or DMC 7457) 1 skein

J = dark autumn gold
Ap 696 (or DMC 7780) 1 skein

K = mid autumn gold
Ap 695 (or DMC 7783) 1 skein

L = light orange-gold
Ap 694 (or DMC 7918) 1 skein

M = pale orange-gold
Ap 693 (or DMC 7173) 1 skein

N = deep olive
Ap 242 (or DMC 7582) 2 skeins

O = light brown-olive
Ap 311 (or DMC 7677) 2 skeins

P = pale drab green
Ap 332 (or DMC 7362) 1 skein

Q = pale olive
Ap 241 (or DMC 7361) 1 skein

R = pale yellow
Ap 471 (or DMC 7472) 1 skein

Note: For alternative yarn brands see *Yarn Alternatives Table* on page 127.

WORKING THE EMBROIDERY

The design covers an area 35 stitches wide by 226 stitches long. Mark the outline of the design (and the grid lines of the chart) onto the canvas, allowing for 6.5cm/2½in of unworked canvas all around the design. If desired, stretch the canvas onto an embroidery frame. (The technical chapter beginning on page 114 gives detailed instructions for marking the canvas, stitching and finishing your needlepoint.)

The chart for the panel is illustrated in two separate sections, but the design should be worked in a continuous strip. Using one strand of tapestry yarn and leaving the background until last, work the design in tent stitch following the chart.

Shading the background

Work the entire embroidery before filling in the background. Work the background mainly with colour B, but speckle it with colour A at random.

BLOCKING AND FINISHING

When the embroidery has been completed, block the canvas as instructed on page 124. Be sure to allow the

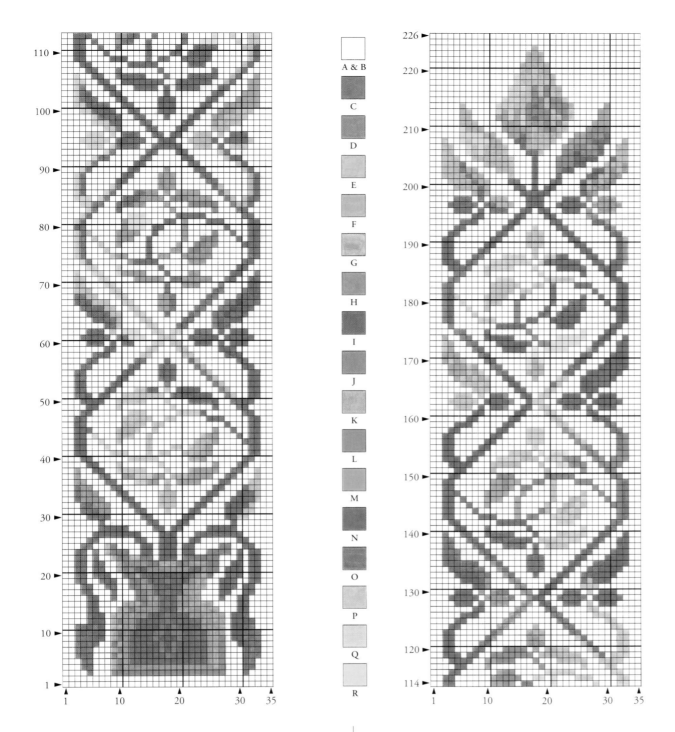

needlepoint to dry completely before removing it from the blocking board or it may distort again.

If you are going to have the needlepoint professionally framed, do not trim the canvas edge until you have had advice from your framer.

Backing the panel

Choose a backing fabric for the panel which matches as closely as possible one of the predominant colours in the needlepoint. It should be of a medium weight, in keeping with the weight of the needlepoint.

Trim the unworked canvas to about 2cm/¾ in all around the edge of the needlepoint.

Press the backing fabric before cutting. Then cut a piece of backing fabric the same size as the trimmed needlepoint canvas.

Turn under the unworked canvas edge all around the embroidery and pin in this position, with the pins perpendicular to the edge so that they can be easily removed once the lining is in place.

Turn the seam allowance on the piece of backing fabric to the wrong side and tack/baste it in position, using a contrasting sewing thread. Press the backing.

Then pin the backing fabric to the panel with the wrong sides together. Using the matching sewing thread and a sewing needle, sew the backing to the needlepoint with small, even slipstitches. Remove the pins and the tacking/basting thread.

CIRCULAR
BIRD STOOL
COVER

*My Circular Bird needlepoint is an adaptation
from a detail in the Book of Kells. It is a more
unusual form than most other Celtic bird patterns.
Two herons – each with foot in mouth – are
arranged in a two-coil spiral. This design is an
excellent example of the balance between nature and
geometric abstraction that is such a hallmark of
Celtic art. Courting a contradiction between nature
and abstraction in this way, Celtic art can unsettle,
astonish or amuse.*

CIRCULAR BIRD
STOOL COVER

SIZE OF NEEDLEPOINT

The finished needlepoint measures 29cm/11½in in diameter or 29cm/11½in square and can be made into a stool cover or, if desired, a cushion/pillow cover.

MATERIALS

10-mesh single-thread canvas 42cm/16½in square

❖

Size 18 tapestry needle

❖

APPLETON Tapestry Wool (*or* PATERNA/YAN *Persian Yarn*) *in the following 17 colours:*

A = wine red
Ap 716 (or Pa 310) 1 skein

B = dark autumn gold
Ap 695 (or Pa 731) 2 skeins

C = mid autumn gold
Ap 694 (or Pa 732) 2 skeins

D = lavender
Ap 885 (or Pa 313) 2 skeins

E = pale lavender
Ap 884 (or Pa 314) 2 skeins

F = light hyacinth blue
Ap 892 (or Pa 343) 1 skein

G = mid hyacinth blue
Ap 894 (or Pa 341) 1 skein

H = dark burgundy
Ap 149 (or Pa 900) 1 skein

I = deep coral
Ap 866 (or Pa 861) 2 skeins

J = coral
Ap 863 (or Pa 862) 1 skein

K = dull coral
Ap 854 (or Pa 802) 1 skein

L = dark mauve
Ap 455 (or Pa 311) 1 skein

M= rose pink
Ap 755 (or Pa 931) 1 skein

N = dusky red
Ap 204 (or Pa 484) 1 skein

O = olive
Ap 342 (or Pa 643) 2 skeins

P = pale yellow
Ap 841 (or Pa 745) 1 skein

Q = mid mauve
Ap 453 (or Pa 300) 1 skein

❖

Note: For alternative yarn brands see *Yarn Alternatives Table* on page 127.

WORKING THE EMBROIDERY

The design covers a circular area 118 stitches wide by 116 stitches tall. Mark the outline of the design (and the grid lines of the chart) onto the canvas, allowing for 6.5cm/2½in of unworked canvas all around the design. If desired, stretch the canvas onto an embroidery frame. (The technical chapter beginning on page 114 gives detailed instructions for marking the canvas, stitching and finishing your needlepoint.)

Using one strand of Appleton tapestry yarn (or three strands of Paterna/yan Persian yarn), work the design in tent stitch following the chart and working the shaded areas as explained below.

Shading

A few areas of the design are shaded. The outline of the birds' necks are shaded in colours B (dark autumn gold) and C (mid autumn gold), and the necks are shaded in colours I (deep coral) and J (coral). The background around the birds' heads and necks is shaded in colours D (lavender) and E (pale lavender). It is not necessary to follow the chart square for square when working these shaded areas. Instead the two shades can be worked in random streaks.

Filling in the corners

You can make the needlepoint square by filling in the corners with random streaks of two shades of your choice. If you do this, you may need to purchase a little extra needlepoint yarn.

BLOCKING AND FINISHING

When the embroidery has been completed, block the canvas as instructed on page 124. Be sure to allow the needlepoint to dry completely before removing it from the blocking board.

If you are having the needlepoint stretched onto a stool, do not trim the canvas as this should be left to the furniture maker making the stool.

Making a cushion cover

If you are making the stool cover into a cushion/pillow cover, you will need to purchase fabric for backing, matching sewing thread, a cushion pad/pillow form the same size as the blocked needlepoint and, if desired, a ready-made cord for edging. You will also need a zipper 3cm/1in shorter than the width of the finished cushion/pillow cover.

After blocking, trim the unworked canvas to about 2cm/¾in all around the edge of the needlepoint.

Using the blocked needlepoint as your template, cut two pieces of backing fabric each half the size of the trimmed canvas and with an extra seam allowance of 2cm/¾in at the centre edge.

Insert the zipper between the two pieces of the backing as instructed on page 125. Complete as instructed on page 125 and sew on the ready-made cord.

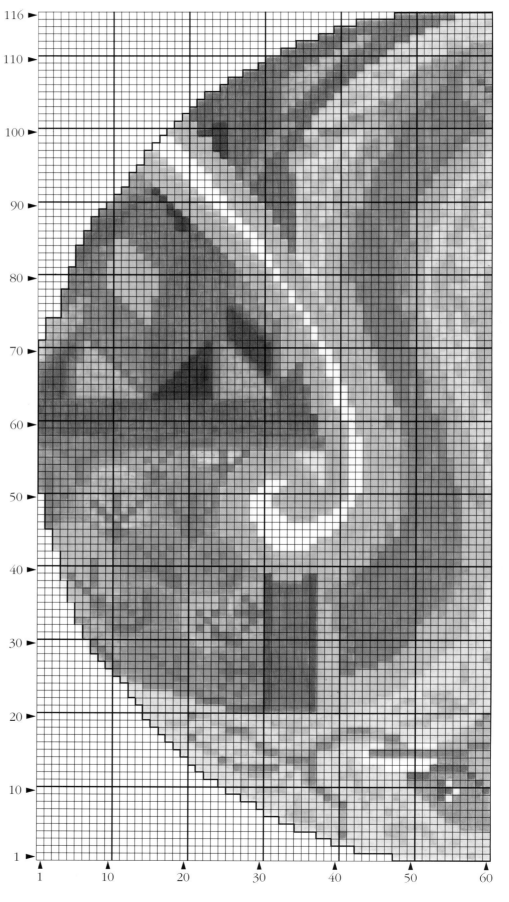

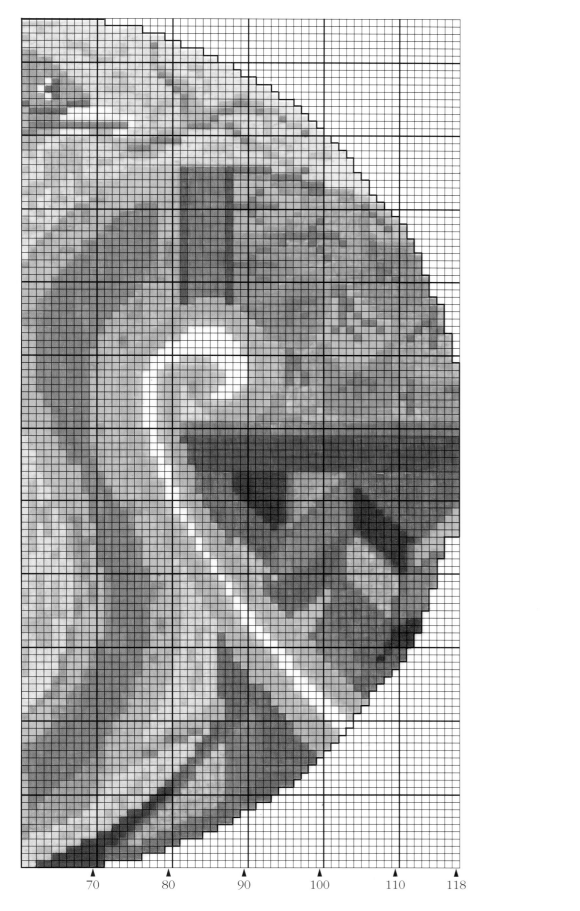

70   80   90   100   110   118

ANIMAL PATTERNS

BEAST-HEAD BELT

The Celtic balance between nature and abstraction captivates me most when I see plain geometry mutating into the forms of fantastic creatures. I designed the Beast-head Belt so that the key pattern – worked in golds – explodes at each end into raging dragon heads. When the belt is fastened at the front, the heads are in full focus, guarding the buckle. As with the Knotwork Belt (see page 64), the regular, repeating key pattern allows the belt to be made to fit any waist size.

BEAST-HEAD
BELT

SIZE OF NEEDLEPOINT

The finished belt measures 5cm/2in wide by the desired length.

Note: The belt pictured measures approximately 68cm/26in long. The recommended yarn amounts, however, are generous and are enough for a much longer belt.

MATERIALS

18-mesh single-thread canvas 18cm/7in wide by the desired finished belt length plus 17cm/6½in extra

❖

Size 22 tapestry needle

❖

Small amount of fabric for belt backing and matching sewing thread

❖

Belt buckle in two parts

❖

ANCHOR *Stranded Cotton embroidery thread/floss (or DMC Stranded Cotton embroidery thread/floss) in the following 12 colours:*

A = navy
An 127 (or DMC 823) 3 skeins

B = dark blue
An 134 (or DMC 820) 3 skeins

C = mid blue
An 132 (or DMC 797) 4 skeins

D = dark rust
An 309 (or DMC 780) 3 skeins

E = rust
An 901 (or DMC 435) 3 skeins

F = gold
An 874 (or DMC 834) 3 skeins

G = light gold
An 887 (or DMC 3046) 3 skeins

H = pink
An 39 (or DMC 309) 1 skein

I = purple
An 100 (or DMC 327) 1 skein

J = dark green
An 216 (or DMC 367) 1 skein

K = green
An 208 (or DMC 562) 1 skein

L = pale fawn
An 391 (or DMC 842) 1 skein

❖

Note: See page 126 for yarn buying information and suppliers addresses.

CALCULATING BELT LENGTH

In order to calculate how long to work the needlepoint belt, first decide on the finished length you will need in order to encompass the waist comfortably. Then subtract the length of the belt buckle. To this result, add 4cm/1½in so that there is an allowance for a turn back of 2cm/¾in at each end of the belt. This will give you the total length required for the needlepoint.

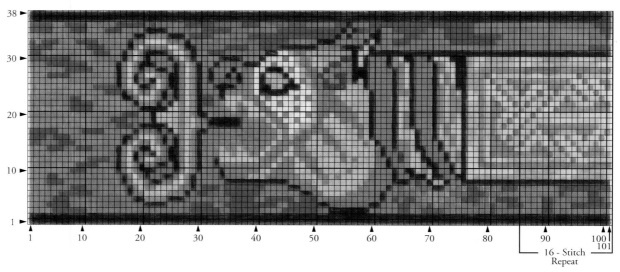

WORKING THE EMBROIDERY

The design covers an area 38 stitches tall by the desired length (see above for calculating length).

Mark the outline of the design (and the grid lines of the chart) onto the canvas, allowing for 6.5cm/2½in of unworked canvas all around the design. If desired, stretch the canvas onto an embroidery frame. (The technical chapter beginning on page 114 gives instructions for marking the canvas, stitching and finishing.)

The chart for the belt is illustrated in two separate sections, but the design should be worked in a continuous strip. Using six strands of the stranded cotton embroidery thread/floss, work the design in tent stitch following the chart and shading as explained below.

Begin by working the left-hand end of the belt and the first 16-stitch key pattern repeat. Then repeat the 16-stitch pattern repeat until the belt measures 13cm/5in shorter than the desired finished length and complete the belt by working the right-hand end.

Shading

Although the chart shows exactly how the belt background(colours B and C) and the key pattern (colours D and E, and F and G) have been shaded, it is not necessary to follow the chart square for square for the shading as long as the shades are sprinkled together in the same manner (see page 123).

BLOCKING AND FINISHING

When the embroidery has been completed, block the canvas as instructed on page 124. Be sure to allow the needlepoint to dry completely before removing it from the blocking board.

Trim the unworked canvas to about 1.5cm/½in all around the edge of the needlepoint.

Backing the belt

Press the fabric gently before cutting. Then cut a piece of backing fabric the same size as the trimmed canvas. Turn under the unworked canvas edge all around the embroidery and pin in this position, with the pins perpendicular to the edge so that they can be easily removed once the lining is in place.

Turn the seam allowance on the piece of backing fabric to the wrong side and tack/baste it in position, using a contrasting sewing thread. Press the backing.

Then pin the backing fabric to the belt with the wrong sides together. Using the matching sewing thread and a sewing needle, sew the backing to the needlepoint with small, even slipstitches. Remove the pins and the tacking/basting thread.

Slip one end of the belt into one part of the buckle, fold under the first fourteen rows of stitches and sew to the wrong side of the belt. Attach the other part of the buckle to the opposite end in the same way.

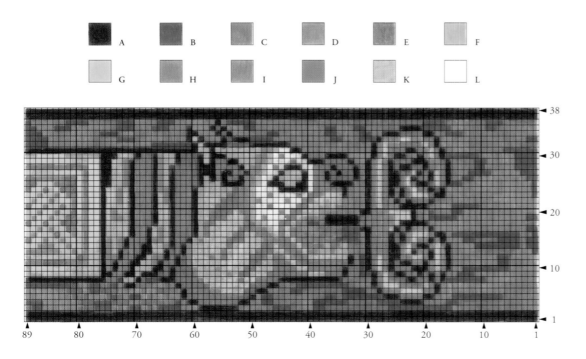

LION AND
LAMB RUG

*The pagan symbol on the Lion and Lamb Rug,
used to illustrate a Christian idea, is not from the
Book of Kells but is totally in the spirit of it.
The theme of this symbol is peace – "and the lion
shall dwell with the lamb". To capture the
spirit of Celtic art, the lion comes more from a
fantastic vision than from reality: its regal purples
and golds evoke the idea of the King of Beasts.
The lamb is deliberately tiny and pale by
comparison. The image is cryptic, bold and
quintessentially Celtic.*

LION AND LAMB
RUG

SIZE OF NEEDLEPOINT

The finished cross stitch rug measures 128cm/50in wide by 82cm/32in tall.

MATERIALS

5-mesh interlock rug canvas 148cm/58in by 96cm/38in

❖

Size 13 tapestry needle

❖

Fabric for backing and matching sewing thread

❖

PATERNA/YAN Persian Yarn in the following 20 colours:

A = charcoal
Paterna shade 221 – 2 hanks

B = dark old blue
Paterna shade 510 – 2 hanks

C = mid old blue
Paterna shade 511 – 2 hanks

D = dark green
Paterna shade 520 – 2 hanks

E = dark marine blue
Paterna shade 530 – 2 hanks

F = mid marine blue
Paterna shade 533 – 2 hanks

G = pale marine blue
Paterna shade 534 – 14 skeins

H = mid grape
Paterna shade 311 – 2½ hanks

I = dark plum
Paterna shade 321 – 2½ hanks

J = dark old gold
Paterna shade 751 – 5 skeins

K = mid old gold
Paterna shade 750 – 1 hank

L = dark verdigris
Paterna shade D511 (or 642) – 1 hank

M = sky blue
Paterna shade 580 – 1 hank

N = deep federal blue
Paterna shade 501 – 1 hank

O = light gold
Paterna shade 742 – 1 hank

P = pale verdigris
Paterna shade D531 (or 753) 1 hank

Q = mid verdigris
Paterna shade D521 (or 752) 1 hank

R = turquoise
Paterna shade 590 – 6 skeins

S = pale ocean green
Paterna shade D546 (or 604) – 14 skeins

T = pale blue
Paterna shade 344 – 1 skein

❖

Note: The "D" shade numbers above are only available in the U.K. An alternative Paterna/yan shade is given in parentheses. For yarn buying information see page 126.

COLOUR MIXTURES

The embroidery for this design is worked using six strands of Paterna/yan Persian yarn. To achieve subtle shading the colours are used singly or in combination. The colour key gives the colour combinations: for example, ABE means two strands each of charcoal, dark old gold and dark marine blue used together, HI means three strands each of mid grape and dark plum used together, and R means six strands of turquoise used together, and so on.

Before threading your needle with a six strand grouping of Persian yarn, separate the strands and then put them together without twisting them.

WORKING THE EMBROIDERY

The design covers an area 251 stitches wide by 161 stitches tall. Mark the outline of the design (and the grid lines of the chart) onto the canvas, allowing for 7.5cm/3in of unworked canvas all around the design.

If desired, stretch the canvas onto an embroidery frame. (The technical chapter beginning on page 114 gives detailed instructions for marking the canvas, stitching and finishing your needlepoint.)

Using six strands of Paterna/yan Persian yarn in the combinations given in the colour key, work the design in cross stitch. Leaving the background until last, begin by working the lion and the lamb.

Stitching the animals

Work the lion and the lamb first, following the chart. Note that the "whites" of the lion's eyes are actually worked in a very pale blue (colour T).

Filling in the background

After completing the lion and the lamb, stitch the background, working the dark part in ABE first and finishing by filling in the light part in CDF.

BLOCKING AND FINISHING

When the embroidery has been completed, if necessary block the canvas as instructed on page 124. Because the embroidery has been worked in cross stitch, it will probably not need blocking. This is because cross stitch does not distort the canvas in the same way that tent stitch does, and because rug canvas tends to be very stable.

Trim the unworked canvas to about 2.5cm/1in all around the needlepoint.

Backing the rug

Cut a piece of backing fabric the same size as the trimmed canvas.

Turn under the unworked canvas edge all around the embroidery and the same amount all around the edge of the backing fabric. Pin the backing fabric to the wrong side of the needlepoint and sew in place.

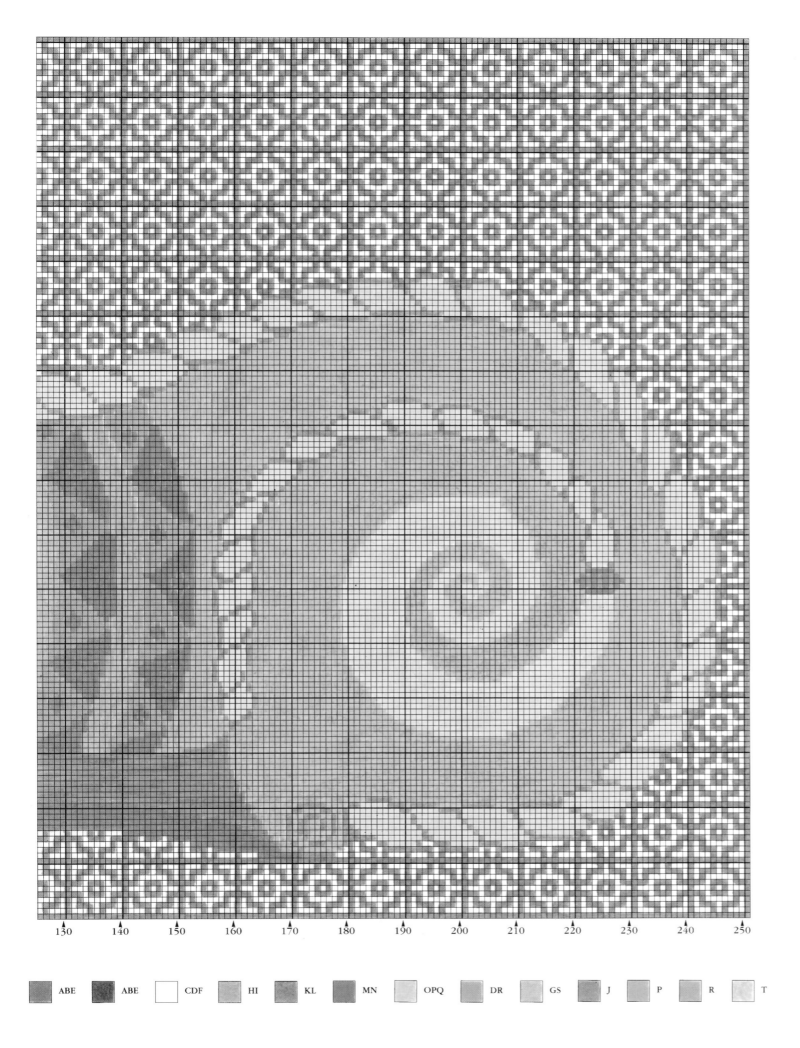

LION TILE
CUSHION

The Lion Tile Cushion *is another faithful rendition of a Celtic symbol. It comes from the same page in the Book of Kells as the* Eagle Tile Cushion *(see page 76) and matches it in spirit and colour. Mark the Evangelist is represented here as a winged lion, contained in circle and square. This depiction of Mark is another supernatural Celtic image used to Christian purpose, and one which perfectly complements the eagle of St. John.*

LION TILE CUSHION

SIZE OF NEEDLEPOINT

The finished needlepoint cushion/pillow measures 42cm/16½in square.

MATERIALS

10-mesh single-thread canvas 55cm/21½in square

Size 18 tapestry needle

Fabric for backing (and if desired, for piping/cording) and matching sewing thread

40cm/16in zipper

1.9m/2yd of ready-made cord or piping cord (optional)

40cm/16in zipper

❖

Cushion pad/pillow form 43cm/17in square

❖

APPLETON Tapestry Wool (or DMC Laine Colbert tapestry yarn) in the following 21 colours:

A = dull mauve
Ap 932 (or DMC 7234) 28m/31yd

B = light dull mauve
Ap 931 (or DMC 7232) 16m/17yd

C = salmon
Ap 143 (or DMC 7226) 17m/19yd

D = cinnamon
Ap 765 (or DMC 7508) 7m/8yd

E = light pink
Ap 142 (or DMC 7223) 19m/20yd

F = deep pink
Ap 146 (or DMC 7208) 24m/26yd

G = dark scarlet
Ap 505 (or DMC 7110) 21m/23yd

H = mid scarlet
Ap 504 (or DMC 7127) 26m/28yd

I = purple
Ap 104 (or DMC 7242) 10m/11yd

J = lavender
Ap 101 (or DMC 7711) 9m/10yd

K = pale lavender
Ap 884 (or DMC 7722) 7m/8yd

L =gold
Ap 843 (or DMC 7473) 28m/31yd

M= light gold
Ap 473 (or DMC 7504) 17m/19yd

N = dark blue
Ap 327 (or DMC 7288) 7m/8yd

O = mid blue
Ap 568 (or DMC 7311) 10m/11yd

P = light blue
Ap 324 (or DMC 7592) 7m/8yd

Q = light fawn
Ap 981 (or DMC 7520) 42m/46yd

R = charcoal
Ap 998 (or DMC 7624) 19m/20yd

S = jade green
Ap 527 (or DMC 7596) 6m/7yd

T = mid green
Ap 293 (or DMC 7394) 13m/14yd

U = pale olive
Ap 241 (or DMC 7361) 28m/31yd

❖

Note: For alternative yarn brands see *Yarn Alternatives Table* on page 127. Hank and skein sizes are given on page 126.

YARN AMOUNTS

The recommended yarn amounts are generous. They are more than enough for working the design in basketweave or continental tent stitch. If your are working the design in half cross stitch, up to 40 per cent less yarn may be needed.

In order to calculate how many skeins of a particular yarn to buy, turn to page 126 for the approximate metrage/yardage per skein. If you are working the design in half cross stitch, you will need about 30 per cent less of each colour.

Also, if the amount required of a particular colour is just over the skein length, it is wise to buy just one skein to start and buy more later only if it is needed. If the amount required is just over the length of two skeins, then buy just two skeins to start, and so on.

Alternatively, you could buy enough skeins to cover the recommended amounts and return any leftover skeins. In this case, check with your yarn shop that they will accept returned yarn.

WORKING THE EMBROIDERY

The design covers an area 167 stitches wide by 166 stitches tall. Mark the outline of the design (and the grid lines of the chart) onto the canvas, allowing for 6.5cm/2½in of unworked canvas all around the design. If desired, stretch the canvas onto an embroidery frame. (The technical chapter beginning on page 114 gives detailed instructions for marking the canvas, stitching and finishing your needlepoint.)

Using one strand of Appleton tapestry yarn (or one strand of DMC Laine Colbert), work the design in tent stitch following the chart.

Shading

It is not necessary to follow the chart square for square in the shaded areas (such as the outer border) as long as the shades are sprinkled together in the same manner (see page 123).

BLOCKING AND FINISHING

When the embroidery has been completed, block the canvas as instructed on page 124. Be sure to allow the needlepoint to dry completely before removing it from the blocking board.

Trim the unworked canvas to about 2cm/¾in all around the edge of the needlepoint.

Backing the cushion

Using the blocked needlepoint as your template, cut two pieces of backing fabric each half the size of the trimmed canvas and with an extra seam allowance of 2cm/¾in at the centre.

Insert the zipper between the two pieces of backing fabric as instructed on page 125.

To make the piping/cording, cut bias strips from the remaining backing fabric and cover the piping/filling cord. Then complete the backing for the cushion/pillow as instructed on page 125.

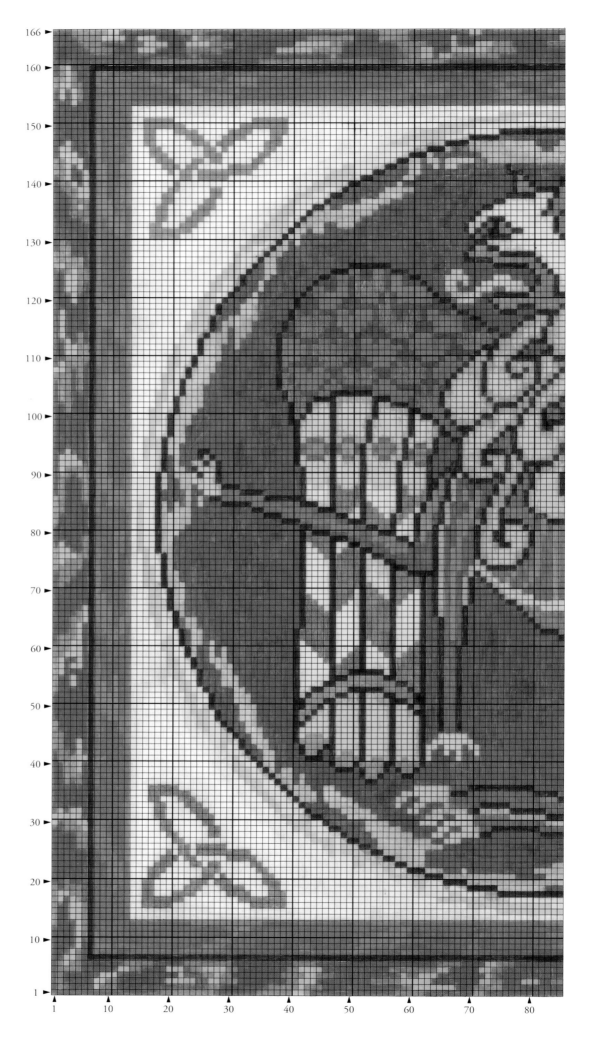

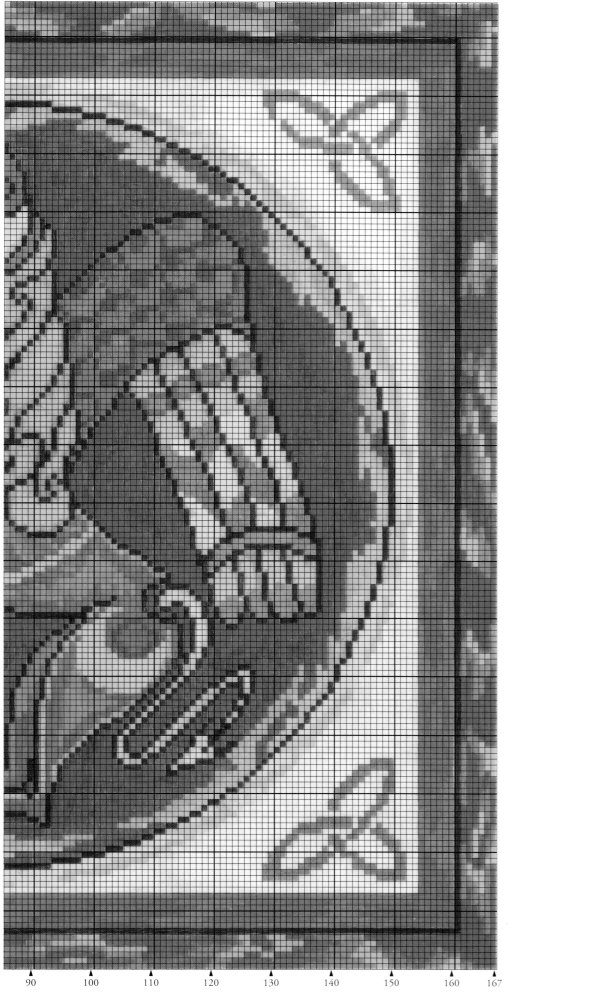

90　　100　　110　　120　　130　　140　　150　　160　167

A
B
C
D
E
F
G
H
I
J
K
L
M
N
O
P
Q
R
S
T
U

NEEDLEPOINT
TECHNIQUES

NEEDLEPOINT
TECHNIQUES

CANVAS

All the embroidery designs in this book are worked on needlepoint canvas, which is a coarse, evenly woven fabric. It is available by the metre/yard, in widths ranging from 45cm/18in to 150cm/60in.

Canvas materials

Needlepoint canvas is made in several different types of material, including cotton, linen, man-made fibres and plastic. Choice of material is largely a matter of personal taste, and high quality polished cotton or linen are my personal preferences.

The most readily available canvas of good quality is made from polished cotton, which is stiffened with sizing to retain its shape. It is strong and durable and suitable for all of the designs in *Celtic Needlepoint*.

Linen canvas is extra hard wearing, less readily available, and considerably more expensive. I would use it for an item which was going to receive very heavy use, or for a needlepoint which I would consider of heirloom quality, such as the *Spiral Chessboard* (see page 42).

Canvas weaves

Needlepoint canvas is available in three different types of weaves as follows:

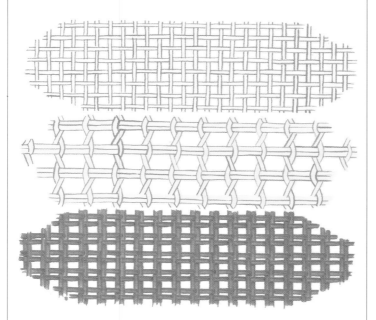

Mono, or single-thread canvas consists of evenly spaced single warp and weft threads (see above, top), and is graded according to the number of threads per inch (see *canvas gauges* below). Single-thread canvas can be used for any needlepoint project, provided the work is not executed in half cross stitch (see page 120). Half cross stitch does not provide the necessary stability to keep the single threads aligned, so continental tent stitch or basketweave tent stitch should always be used to achieve the same look as half cross stitch on mono canvas.

Interlock canvas is graded like mono canvas, and consists of threads twisted so that the warp and weft threads interlock at the intersections (see illustration, centre). This prevents the threads shifting, making interlock canvas suitable for all types of stitches, including half cross.

The main disadvantage of this type of canvas, with the exception of heavy interlock rug canvas, is that the threads are weak at the intersections, and the canvas tends to pull out of shape. Blocking it back into shape can be difficult as the threads may break if too much force is employed.

Lighter weight interlock canvas is best used for small needlepoint designs which are not destined for hard wear. I would also advise always using an embroidery frame when stitching on interlock canvas, as this will ensure that it stays in better shape.

Double-thread or Penelope canvas has double threads for each mesh (see illustration, bottom). Needlepoint stitches are usually worked over pairs of threads. This ensures that the canvas remains strong and stable and can take quite forceful stretching during blocking if necessary.

Canvas gauges

Needlepoint canvas is graded according to the number of holes per inch and is generally made in mesh sizes from 22 to 5 holes per inch. The finest gauges are only available in mono canvas and the coarsest only in interlock rug canvas.

Although double-thread canvas can be found in mesh sizes 12 and 14, it is most readily available in mesh sizes of 7 to 10 holes per inch. Because the threads are double, however, it is possible to use a double-thread canvas as a mono canvas with twice the number of holes per inch. For example, a 10-mesh double-thread canvas can be used as a 20-mesh single-thread canvas by working the stitches between the double threads.

It is also possible to work detailed areas in the single gauge (petit point) and the background in the double gauge (gros point), though none of the designs in this book employ this technique.

Canvas colours

Canvas with 10 holes to the inch or heavier is usually available in ecru or white. My preference is to use ecru if the needlepoint is mainly worked in medium to dark shades, and white if it is mainly light or has any appreciable amounts of white in the stitching.

Purchasing canvas

Whatever your choice of canvas, always ensure that you purchase enough to allow for 6cm (2½in) of spare canvas all around the proposed design.

Altering canvas gauge

You may enlarge or reduce any design by working it on a different gauge of canvas to that given. To calculate the finished size of the design on an alternative gauge, divide the number of stitches in the width and length of the project, by the alternative canvas gauge. The result will give you the alternative width and length of the needlepoint.

If you substitute the given canvas with one that has more than one hole fewer per inch, you may need to change the thickness of yarn used, so that the thread will not be difficult to pull through the holes. Likewise, using a gauge larger than the one recommended may mean that you will have to use thicker yarn to cover the canvas adequately. This can be easily done with stranded yarn, simply by reducing the number of strands on the needle.

Please note, however, that I have shaded many of my designs with specific colour combinations of a given number of strands, and changing the number will have some effect on the colour balance. I would recommend that you try out a test sample to check if you like the effect before changing any of these particular designs.

YARNS AND THREADS

There is a large selection of needlepoint yarns available, and many come in an extensive range of colours. I have a strong preference for natural fibres, with wool as my firm favourite. Consequently, I use wool for most of my designs.

Wool yarn for needlepoint is hard wearing and comes in three types:

Crewel wool is a fine, twisted 2-ply yarn which can be used singly on a fine mesh (20 to 22 holes per inch) canvas. On a coarser mesh two or more strands of crewel wool can be used together. The great advantage of crewel wool is that different shades and colours can be combined on the needle to produce subtle effects. This is why I prefer to use crewel over any other type of needlepoint yarn.

Tapestry wool is a 4-ply yarn, thus producing a thick single thread suitable for use singly on a 10- to 12-mesh canvas, or doubled on a 5- to 6-mesh canvas.

Persian yarn is a lustrous yarn which comes in triple strands. Though it is a slightly heavier weight than crewel, it can also be used in single strands or in any combination of number and colour to suit canvas and design. It is important to remember that when using more or less than three strands of Persian yarn together, regardless of colour, you must separate the strands and put them together again on the needle, without twisting them together. This will ensure that the subsequent stitches will lie smoothly.

Yarn amounts

The instructions on the preceding pages specify the amount of yarn you will need in each colour. These recommended amounts are generous, especially when random shading has been used in the design (see *shading* on page 123).

Note: More information about wool needlepoint yarns and cotton and silk threads is given on page 126.

NEEDLEPOINT TOOLS AND EQUIPMENT

When making a needlepoint design, you will need the usual needlework tools for finishing. The tools and equipment mentioned here are those needed specifically when working the embroidery.

Tapestry needles

Tapestry needles should always be used for stitching needlepoints. They have a long eye and a rounded tip and are available in a variety of sizes. The required needle size is given in the instructions for each project in the book, though generally speaking, the eye should be large enough to take the yarn freely, and the needle itself should draw the yarn smoothly through the canvas. The illustration below shows a range of tapestry needles and yarns.

Frames

Needlepoint can be worked with or without the use of an embroidery frame. I always use a frame, as I find that the time spent setting up is well worth the effort, and indeed, is more than compensated for in speed gained during stitching and finishing.

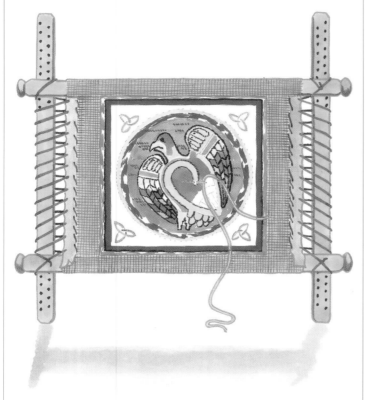

The first advantage of the frame is that it keeps the canvas taut. A good frame, such as the slate frame (see above), is strong enough to maintain the canvas shape throughout the stitching, and thus eliminates the need to stretch the work on completion.

Another great bonus, is that both hands are free to move the needle back and forth through the canvas. I am right-handed and I move the needle down through the top of the canvas with my right hand and catch it underneath and move it up through the bottom with my left hand. I find this really speeds up the process. This works particularly well when the embroidery frame is on a stand and therefore does not need to be held.

Some stitchers prefer to work without a frame. The main advantage is that this makes the work much more portable. The disadvantages are that it is more difficult to keep an even tension on the stitches, and unless you are working in cross stitch, the canvas will distort considerably as the piece

is stitched. It will have to be stretched back into shape when the work is completed (see page 124 for *blocking*).

Scissors

You will require two pairs of sharp scissors, one for cutting the canvas to size, and one small pointed pair, or clippers to cut the yarn and trim the finished ends during stitching (see illustration below).

Marker pens

I use indelible pens (see below) to mark the outline and guidelines on the canvas. I would advise always checking to make sure that the ink is indelible and will not run when wet. To do this, I mark a small piece of canvas, allowing the pen marks to dry for roughly ten minutes, then wet the marked canvas. If the ink does not run at all, then it is safe to use. I use a medium ochre and grey for marking ecru canvas and a pale ochre and light grey for white canvas. (See page 121 for *marking the canvas*.)

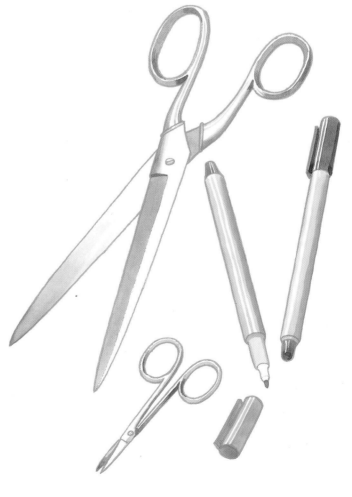

STITCHES

There are many different stitches used in needlepoint as a whole. I have chosen to use only a few which suit the particular designs in this book, and they are all illustrated here.

Tent stitch (continental)

Continental tent stitch is the most commonly used of all needlepoint stitches, and I have found it is the best stitch to use for most of my Celtic needlepoint designs. It allows for easy shading (see page 123), and shows detail well. It is also very hard wearing as the long stitches on the reverse form a dense backing which protects the work.

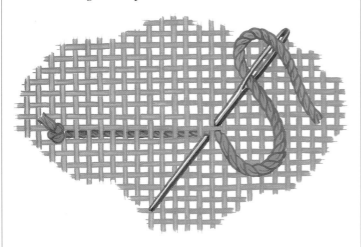

To begin stitching, tie a knot at the end of the thread and insert the needle from front to back through the canvas a few stitches along and in the path of the stitches to be worked, so that the knot lies on the top surface. Then bring the needle up at the lower left-hand corner of the first stitch to be worked. Take the needle over one canvas intersection and insert it through the canvas diagonally from right to left as shown above. Continue in this way (see below) from

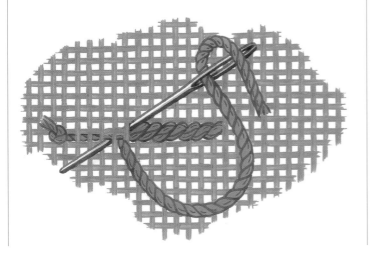

right to left across the row of stitches, inserting the needle in the same way for each of the stitches. When a few continental tent stitches have been worked over the starting thread at the back of the canvas, clip the knot carefully as the end will now be firmly anchored.

To finish off a thread, pass it through the back of the stitches just worked for roughly 2.5cm/1in and carefully clip off the end.

Basketweave tent stitch

Basketweave tent stitch is, in effect, the same stitch as continental tent stitch and both stitches can be used on the same canvas. The basketweave technique can only be used efficiently on large continuous areas, such as the background of the *Hexagonal Knotwork Cushion* (see page 58). The stitch is undoubtedly named for the basketweave effect created on the reverse of the canvas. This effect has the added advantage of helping prevent the canvas from becoming very distorted (or biased). I would therefore specially recommend it if you are working large areas and not using a frame.

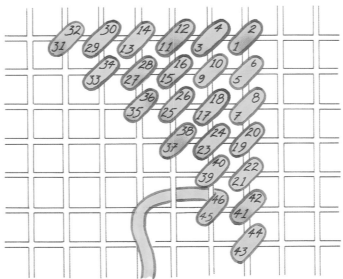

To begin stitching, tie a knot at the end of the thread and insert the needle from front to back through the canvas a few stitches along and in the path of the stitches to be worked as explained for continental tent stitch. Work the second stitch as for continental tent stitch, but bring the needle up one intersection below the first stitch. The rows of stitches are worked diagonally, alternately upwards and downwards. The numbers in the diagram above show the path of the needle.

basketweave tent stitch. However, this also means that the resulting embroidery is thinner, having short, straight stitches on the back. This makes a half cross stitch needlepoint a good deal less hard wearing and I would recommend it only for work which will not receive too much wear.

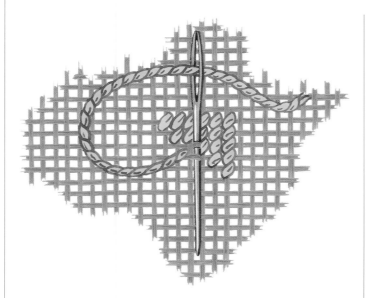

On the downward diagonal journey the needle is repeatedly inserted vertically under two canvas threads (above).

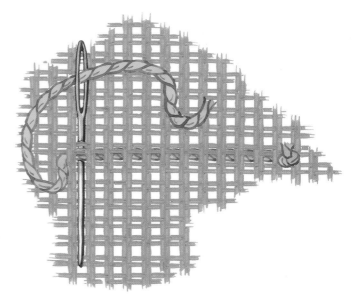

To begin half cross stitch, secure the thread end as for continental tent stitch, bringing the needle up at the lower left-hand corner of the first stitch. Take the thread over one canvas intersection and insert the needle vertically through the canvas as shown above.

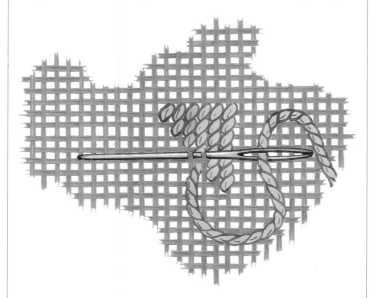

On the upward diagonal journey the needle is repeatedly inserted horizontally under two canvas threads (above).

The downward and upward journey are worked alternately until the required area of canvas has been filled. The thread is finished off as for continental tent stitch.

Half cross stitch

The half cross stitch technique can be substituted for the other tent stitch techniques, provided you use a double-thread or interlock canvas. The advantage of half cross stitch is that it distorts the canvas less than continental tent stitch and uses up to forty per cent less yarn than continental or

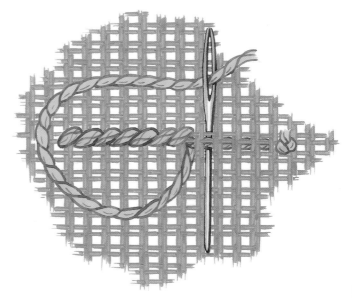

Working over the thread end to secure it, work each stitch in the same way from left to right (see above). Secure the thread end as for continental tent stitch.

Cross stitch

Cross stitch produces a very distinctive texture due to the fact that each cross forms a complete square rather than the single diagonal line of half cross, continental and basketweave tent stitches.

Because each stitch crosses in both directions, cross stitch does not create any canvas distortion. For this reason it can be worked easily without a frame. Cross stitch is also very dense, which makes it a perfect stitch for rugs.

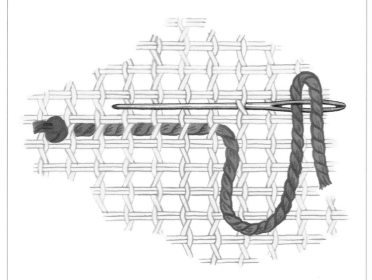

To begin stitching, knot the end of the thread and insert the needle from front to back through the canvas a few stitches along and in the path of the stitches to be worked as for continental tent stitch. Then bring the needle up at the lower left-hand corner of the first stitch to be worked. Take the needle over one canvas intersection and insert it through the canvas from right (see above). Next (see below) insert

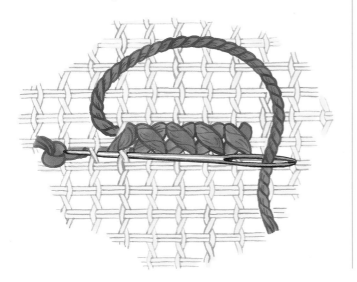

the needle from right to left through the canvas at the bottom of the stitch, bringing it out one canvas intersection to the left in the position to begin the next stitch. Continue in this way from right to left across the row of stitches. To finish off the thread, pass it through the back of the stitches just worked as for the various forms of tent stitch.

When working cross stitch designs, it is very important to make sure that all the top stitches of the crosses lie in the same direction in order to ensure a smooth texture.

WORKING FROM CHARTS

Though working from charts may seem a daunting prospect to the newcomer, the one great advantage they have over a printed canvas is that there is no doubt as to exactly where each stitch lies. This is particularly important if the design is composed of accurate geometric shapes, as is the case in many of the projects here. In fact, they can only be worked successfully from charts or on carefully hand-painted canvases (see page 128 for *kit information*).

Every square on a tent-stitch (or cross-stitch) needlepoint chart represents a single stitch on the canvas. It is essential to understand that as the stitches are formed on the threads of the canvas, the squares in the chart are translated onto the thread intersections of the canvas, not the holes. To anchor this concept firmly in my mind, I always think of the horizontal rows of squares on the chart as the horizontal threads (weft) of the canvas, and the vertical rows, as the vertical threads (warp) of the canvas.

Marking the canvas

The main problem many stitchers encounter with charts, is keeping track of exactly where they are at any point. I use a method of marking the canvas before I begin, so that I can very quickly tell where any stitch should be placed.

To mark the canvas I use two different colours of indelible pen (see *marker pens* on page 118) – one for the outline, and one for the grid lines.

It is vital to ensure that you mark the grid lines accurately, as they will be the guidelines for stitching while following the chart. The best way to explain how to do this is by example. The basis for the marked needlepoint canvas on the following pages is the chart for the *Spiral Sewing Case* on page 51.

Lay the cut canvas flat on a table and place the chart within easy sight, so that the chart and canvas are placed in the same direction, i.e. width and length matching. I place a polythene sheet, or newspaper under the canvas to protect the table from ink stains. Measure up 6cm/2½ in from the bottom of the canvas, and with the outline colour pen, make a small mark on a *horizontal thread* this distance from the edge. Then make a small mark on a *vertical thread* 6cm/2½ in from the left edge of the canvas. These marked threads (see right) will be the bottom outline and the left outline. They represent the bottom horizontal row of the chart and the first vertical row at the far left of the chart.

Next, using the contrasting marker pen, mark the thread after each tenth vertical row of stitches. Counting the marked left-hand edge outline thread as the first stitch, count ten threads along and mark the next vertical thread. Then, counting the last marked thread as number one, again count ten threads along and mark the next vertical thread. Continue in this

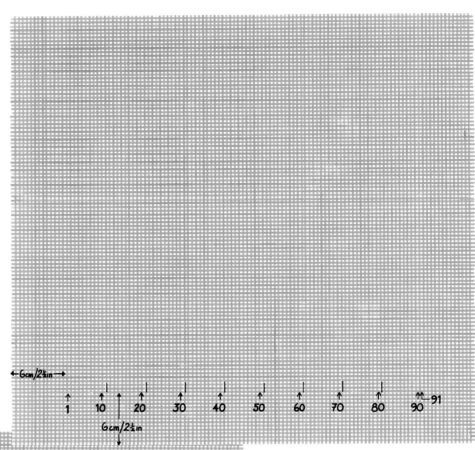

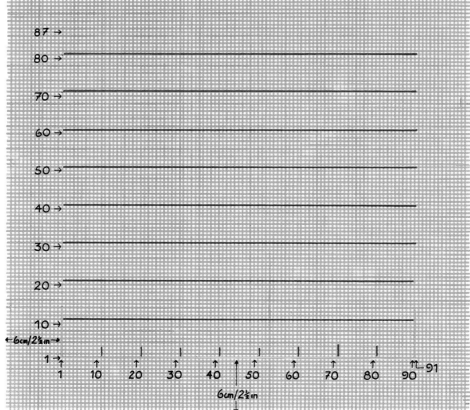

way across the bottom of the canvas as shown above. To ensure total accuracy, check each count of ten as you proceed. The last vertical row of stitches on the *Spiral Sewing Case* is the ninety-first row, so this becomes the right outline on the canvas (see above). Mark the right outline thread with the outline colour pen.

Once all the grid lines have been marked along the bottom of the canvas, you can complete the bottom outline. Using a ruler and the outline pen, mark the bottom outline along its entire length. To mark the horizontal grid lines, begin at the bottom, counting the bottom outline as the first row. Using the contrasting pen, mark the horizontal grid positions as for the vertical ones (see left), then mark the horizontal grid lines across the entire

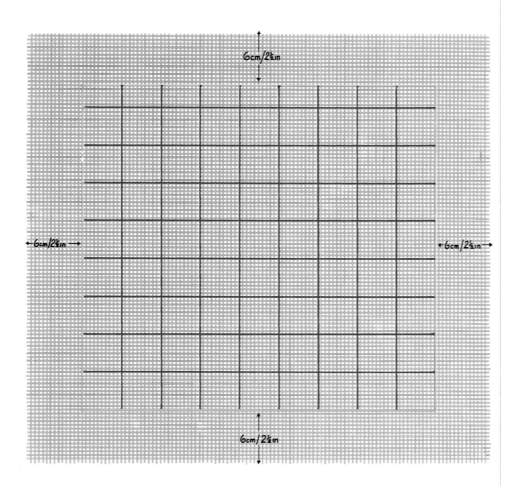

design. Counting the last grid line as number one, count up seven threads and mark the seventh thread with the outline pen. This top outline represents the last row of the chart as shown in the illustration at the bottom of the opposite page.

Still using the outline pen, extend the right and left outline and mark the entire length of the top outline. Then, using the contrasting pen, extend the vertical grid lines. This completes the marking of the canvas (see above).

From chart to canvas

You are now ready to begin stitching. The important concept to grasp is that the horizontal grid lines on the canvas represent the first row of squares *above* the chart grid line, and the vertical grid lines on the canvas represent the row of squares on the immediate *right* of the chart grid lines. It is now easy to identify the position of any stitch from chart to canvas. For example, if you want to work a particular stitch, count in which "ten square" the stitch lies and then count on the canvas from the horizontal grid line upwards, and from the vertical grid lines to the right. You can pinpoint any stitch in this way and you are free to skip around the needlepoint, working any area you wish.

Rotating a chart

For needlepoints which show a half or quarter chart, mark only the half or quarter shown on the chart. These designs will all be either symmetrical or rotate. Once you have stitched the first quarter (or half), the rest of the design is easily followed by referring to the area already stitched.

SHADING

Many of the needlepoints in this book are composed of design patterns which are subtly shaded at random. The charts show shading on the patterned areas, and in some cases, the background is shown unshaded, though you will be required to shade it at random. In these cases, the background is shown as a plain colour for the sake of clarity in reading the chart.

The exact combinations of colours to use for shading are given in the instructions. The easiest and most enjoyable way to shade is to really do it at random, rather than following exactly as shown in the chart. The shading shown on the charts should be regarded as a rough guide as to the size of areas worked in any one colour.

Simple shading

Random two-colour shading adds depth and dimension to the design. For example, I have shaded the plain borders in the *Spiral Chessboard* (see page 42) at random, using two different shades.

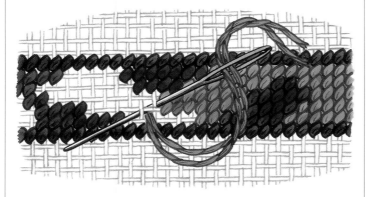

To shade a two-colour border, thread up one colour and work a small area along the border. Then move along and stitch another small area at random. When the thread is used up, take the second colour and fill in the spaces (see above). Continue along the border in this fashion.

Working complex shading

The *Key and Knotwork Footstool Cover* (see page 28) is a good example of more complex shading. Here, the background is randomly shaded using three different colours of crewel wool and all the possible mixtures of all three colours in the one thread. The result is very subtle, and almost organic, and great fun to work.

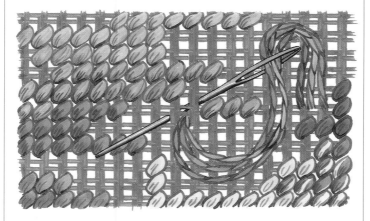

To shade a background with multiple shade variations, begin by working small areas of the solid colours (those worked with three strands of the same shade) spaced some distance apart. Then fill in the spaces with the mixed colours, at random (see above).

BLOCKING

When working continental or basketweave tent stitch or half cross stitch, the diagonal slope of the stitches will gradually pull the canvas out of shape. This will happen to a small degree, even if you do use a frame, especially with large needlepoints. It is necessary to block the canvas in order to fix it back into shape.

To block the needlepoint canvas, you will need a board and a clean cloth, both larger than the canvas. You will also need rust proof carpet tacks, a hammer, a large set-square and a ruler. The board must be soft enough to allow the tacks to stay in place.

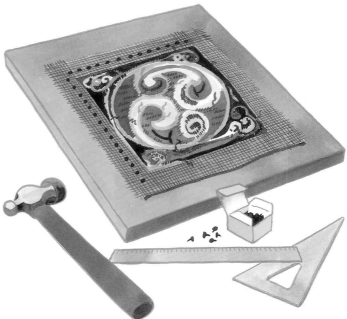

Pin the cloth to the board. Dampen the back of the needlepoint evenly and place it face down on the cloth-covered board. Line up one edge of the needlepoint with a ruler and tack it in place lightly (the tacks will probably need to be moved at a later stage). Place the tacks approximately 12mm/½in apart and 2.5cm/1in from the edge of the needlepoint. Pull the canvas into shape and tack down the adjacent edge (see above), checking with the set-square that the corner is a right angle.

Continue in this manner, dampening the canvas as necessary and pulling it until it is taut and all corners are right angled. You may need to place the final tacks closer together to achieve the right degree of tension. Allow the canvas to dry slowly, away from direct heat, and leave in this position for a minimum of a day and a half.

FINISHING

There are a number of professional finishers who will block and finish off your needlepoints. Although you will probably want to leave framing your needlepoint, or stretching your needlepoint onto custom-built furniture to the professionals, you may prefer to finish simpler items yourself. The individual instructions for the designs in this book include the simpler finishing techniques, such as backing a bookmark, making a glasses case, etc. Making a simple cushion cover is explained here.

Backing fabrics for cushions

Choice of backing fabric is a matter of taste, but a fabric which colour-matches the needlepoint is essential. Remember that the colour you choose will emphasise the colour it matches in the embroidery, especially if you are using the fabric for a cord to frame the design.

Always choose a type and weight of fabric to suit the piece. I have a very strong preference for natural fibres, such as cotton, linen, wool or silk.

If you are going to cover a piping/filling cord, be sure to buy sufficient fabric for the bias strips needed.

Preparing the backing

You can sew the backing to your needlepoint without inserting a zipper, but it is handy to be able to remove the cushion pad/pillow form without cutting open a seam.

The easiest way to sew a zipper to your cover is to insert it into a seam down the centre of the backing. For this you will need to cut two pieces of backing fabric, each half the size of the needlepoint, plus a 2cm/¾in seam allowance all around each piece.

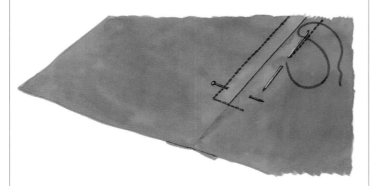

Join each end of the centre seam about 3.5cm/1¼in, leaving the centre of the seam open for the zipper. Pin the zipper to the wrong side of the backing fabric, and sew it in place by hand or using a sewing machine with a zipper foot (see above). Press the right side of the seam. Set the prepared backing aside until the piping/cording is ready.

Making piping/cording

You may want to make piping/cording to match your backing if you cannot find a suitable ready-made cord or if a ready-made cord would detract from the design.

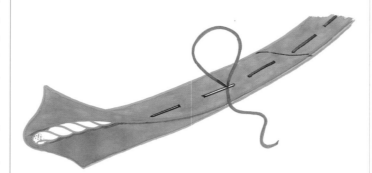

First, cut bias strips wide enough to cover the cord and to allow for a 2cm/¾in seam allowance on each side. Seaming the strips on the diagonal (with the grain of the fabric), join enough strips to cover the entire length of the cord. Fold the strip around the cord and tack/baste in place close to the cord (see above).

Sewing on the backing

Once you have prepared the piping and backing, you can sew them to the needlepoint.

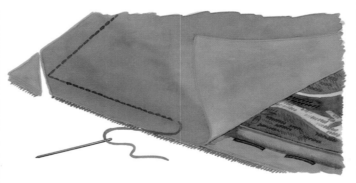

First, pin the piping all around the edge of the needlepoint lining the seam allowance up with the seam allowance on the canvas and turning the ends towards the raw edges of the seam where they meet. The row of tacking/basting stitches on the piping/cording should line up with the edge of the embroidery (see above). Then place the backing on top of the needlepoint with right sides together and pin it in place. Sew the backing and the piping/cording to the needlepoint, using backstitch or using a sewing machine with a zipper foot. Clip the corners diagonally (see above) and trim the seam allowance slightly to neaten it. Turn right side out and insert the cushion pad/pillow form.

YARN AND KIT INFORMATION

Buying Yarns and Threads

All of the instructions for the projects in this book (except for the instructions for the *Lion and Lamb Rug* and the *Key Pattern Glasses Case*) give a choice of two embroidery yarn/thread brands. The first brand mentioned in the instructions is the recommended brand and is the brand used by the author. The yarn given in parentheses is the suggested alternative (further alternatives are given below in the *Yarn Alternatives Table*). If you use an alternative yarn, the colours will not be exactly the same as the original yarn, so it is best, when possible, to use the recommended brand.

Shade numbers

The colour descriptions in the instructions are given as a general guide and are not necessarily the names given by the yarn manufacturers. When ordering yarn, always quote the shade numbers given in the instructions.

Yarn amounts

Every effort has been made to ensure that the yarn amounts quoted in this book are sufficient. For this reason, the amounts given in the instructions are generous and will be sufficient for an embroidery worked entirely in continental tent stitch. If you use the half cross stitch technique rather than the continental tent stitch technique, you may find that you use as much as 20 to 30 per cent less than the yarn amounts quoted.

The yarn amounts recommended for the designs worked in random shading are particularly generous as no two stitchers will work the random streaks in exactly the same way. When buying yarn for these designs, it is wise to make sure that excess hanks are returnable.

Yarn Brands

The following are the embroidery yarns/threads either used for the designs in this book or quoted as alternatives. The lengths given for skeins and hanks are approximate. When buying very large amounts it is best to buy hanks, if possible, instead of skeins. (Read *Buying Yarns and Threads* above, before calculating yarn amounts needed. See also page 78 about calculating the number of skeins or hanks required.)

Ap = APPLETON *Crewel Wool*
25m/27yd per skein
182m/200yd per hank
APPLETON *Tapestry Wool*
10m/11yd per skein
55m/60yd per hank

Pa = PATERNA/YAN *Persian Yarn*
three 7.4m/8yd strands per skein
three 155m/170yd strands per 4oz hank

Note: When Persian yarn is given as an alternative to crewel wool for a design, the metrage/yardage specified is for a single strand. Therefore, when you are calculating how many skeins or hanks to buy for this type of needlepoint design, the skein or hank lengths quoted above should be multiplied by three.

DMC = DMC *Médicis*
25m/27yd per skein
DMC *Laine Colbert*
8m/8¼yd per skein
DMC *Stranded Cotton*
six 8m/9yd strands per skein

An = ANCHOR *Tapestry Wool*
10m/11yd per skein
ANCHOR *Stranded Cotton*
six 8m/9yd strands per skein

Kr = KREINIK *Soie d'Algers*
seven 5m/5½yd strands per skein
(available in 400 shades)

Appleton tapestry wool, DMC Laine Colbert and Anchor tapestry wool are all 100 per cent wool "tapestry weight" needlepoint yarns and one strand is sufficient for working on a 10-mesh canvas.

Appleton crewel wool, DMC Médicis and Paterna/yan Persian yarn are all finer wool yarns. Three or four strands of crewel wool, three strands of Medicis, and two or three strands of Persian yarn are sufficient for working tent stitch on a 10-mesh canvas.

Note: When using three strands of Persian yarn on a 10-mesh canvas, you should work on a single-thread canvas.

Yarn Alternatives Table

Although one alternative brand is offered (in parentheses) in each set of instructions, the following designs could also be worked in the alternatives listed below. (See also, *Buying Yarns and Threads* above.)

page 16 **Key Pattern Cushion**
DMC *Médicis* in the following colours could be used as an approximate substitute:
A = DMC 8400
B = DMC 8484
C = DMC 8303
D = DMC 8896
E = DMC 8895
F = DMC 8122
G = DMC 8107
H = DMC 8418
I = DMC 8419
J = DMC 8214
K = DMC 8504
L = DMC 8505

page 24 **Key and Knotwork Workbox Cover**
DMC *Médicis* in the following colours could be used as an approximate substitute:
A = DMC 8201
B = DMC 8203
C = DMC 8305
D = DMC 8400
E = DMC 8324

page 30 **Key and Knotwork Footstool Cover**
DMC *Médicis* in the following colours could be used as an approximate substitute:
A = DMC 8332
B = DMC 8895
C = DMC 8208
D = DMC 8400
E = DMC 8214
F = DMC 8426

page 38 **Spiral Cushion**
DMC *Médicis* in the following colours could be used as an approximate substitute:
A = DMC 8404
B = DMC 8410
C = DMC 8426
D = DMC 8997
E = DMC 8996
F = DMC 8407
G = DMC 8313
H = DMC 8303
I = DMC 8484
J = DMC 8114
K = DMC 8102
L = DMC 8103
M = DMC 8126
N = DMC 8127
O = DMC 8104

page 60 Hexagonal Knotwork Cushion

Three strands of PATERNA/YAN *Persian Yarn* or one strand of ANCHOR *Tapestry Wool* in the following colours could be used as an approximate substitute:

A = Pa 510 or An 8838
B = Pa 530 or An 8906
C = Pa 202 or An 9776
D = Pa 472 or An 9620

page 66 Knotwork Belt

DMC *Médicis* in the following colours could be used as an approximate substitute:

A = DMC NOIR
B = DMC 8204
C = DMC 8380

page 70 Knotwork Carpet Seat Cushion

DMC *Médicis* in the following colours could be used as an approximate substitute:

A = DMC 8103
B = DMC 8126
C = DMC 8127
D = DMC 8304
E = DMC 8484
F = DMC 8303

page 78 Eagle Tile Cushion

Three strands of PATERNA/YAN *Persian Yarn* or one strand of ANCHOR *Tapestry Wool* in the following colours could be used as an approximate substitute:

A = Pa 472 or An 9598
B = Pa 433 or An 9620
C = Pa 922 or An 8508
D = Pa 495 or An 9448
E = Pa 923 or An 8506
F = Pa 910 or An 8424
G = Pa 900 or An 8220
H = Pa 968 or An 8442
I = Pa 311 or An 8592
J = Pa 312 or An 8588
K = Pa 314 or An 8584
L = Pa 733 or An 8020
M = Pa 734 or An 8018
N = Pa 327 or An 8838
O = Pa 501 or An 8794
P = Pa 512 or An 8738
Q = Pa 464 or An 9654
R = Pa 221 or An 9768
S = Pa 534 or An 8832
T = Pa 602 or An 9066
U = Pa 653 or An 9304
V = Pa 530 or An 8906

page 84 Interlaced Heron Bookmark

ANCHOR *Stranded Cotton* in the following colours could be used as an approximate substitute:

A = An 874 – light gold
B = An 304 – orange
C = An 242 – green
D = An 433 – bright blue
E = An 47   – dark crimson
F = An 334 – scarlet
G = An 337 – musk
H = An 164 – dark blue
    An 879 – dark green

page 88 Tree of Life Panel

Three strands of PATERNA/YAN *Persian Yarn* or one strand of ANCHOR *Tapestry Wool* in the following colours could be used as an approximate substitute:

A = Pa 510 or An 8794
B = Pa 501 or An 8822
C = Pa 910 or An 8424
D = Pa 922 or An 8508
E = Pa 923 or An 8506
F = Pa 924 or An 9636
G = Pa 485 or An 9512
H = Pa 931 or An 8348
I = Pa 730 or An 8064
J = Pa 731 or An 8102
K = Pa 732 or An 8100
L = Pa 497 or An 9446
M = Pa 498 or An 9444
N = Pa 651 or An 9216
O = Pa 752 or An 9286
P = Pa 643 or An 9258
Q = Pa 653 or An 9304
R = Pa 743 or An 8054

page 92 Circular Bird Stool Cover

DMC *Laine Colbert* or ANCHOR *Tapestry Wool* in the following colours could be used as an approximate substitute:

A = DMC 7259 or An 8514
B = DMC 7782 or An 8024
C = DMC 7473 or An 8042
D = DMC 7709 or An 8588
E = DMC 7722 or An 8586
F = DMC 7283 or An 8604
G = DMC 7555 or An 8608
H = DMC 7219 or An 8426
I = DMC 7920 or An 8240
J = DMC 7875 or An 8234
K = DMC 7918 or An 8166
L = DMC 7242 or An 8592
M = DMC 7195 or An 8400

N = DMC 7166 or An 8328
O = DMC 7373 or An 9054
P = DMC 7905 or An 8052
Q = DMC 7895 or An 8590

page 110 Lion Tile Cushion

Three strands of PATERNA/YAN *Persian Yarn* or one strand of ANCHOR *Tapestry Wool* in the following colours could be used as an approximate substitute:

A – R and T and U as for **Eagle Tile Cushion** above

S = Pa 527 or An 8922

YARN SUPPLIERS ADDRESSES

The embroidery yarns/threads used in this book are widely available in specialist needlework shops and in large department stores. To find a stockist near you, see below; or contact the yarn companies or the yarn distributors listed here.

APPLETON YARN
U.K.

APPLETON BROS LTD, Thames Works, Church Street, Chiswick, London W4 2PE, England. Tel: (081) 994 0711. Fax: 081 995 6609.

Stockists in U.S.A.

ACCESS DISCOUNT COMMODITIES, PO Box 156, Simpsonville, Maryland 21150.
CHAPARRAL, 3701 West Alabama, Suite 370, Houston, Texas 77027.
DAN'S FIFTH AVENUE, 1520 Fifth Avenue, Canyon, Texas 79015.
THE ELEGANT NEEDLE LTD, 7945 MacArthur Boulevard, Suite 203, Cabin John, Maryland 20818.
EWE TWO LTD, 24 North Merion Avenue, Bryn Mawr, Pennsylvania 19010.
FLEUR DE PARIS, 5835 Washington Boulevard, Culver City, California 90230.
HANDCRAFT FROM EUROPE, PO Box 31524, San Francisco, California 94131-0524.
THE JOLLY NEEDLEWOMAN, 5810 Kennett Pike, Centreville Delaware 19807.
LOUISE'S NEEDLEWORK, 45 North High Street, Dublin, Ohio 43017.
NATALIE, 144 North Larchmont Boulevard, Los Angeles, California 90004.
NEEDLEPOINT INC, 251 Post Street, 2nd Floor, San Francisco, California 94108.
NEEDLE WORKS LTD, 4041 Tulane Avenue, New Orleans, Louisiana 70119.
POTPOURRI ETC, PO Box 78, Redondo Beach, California 90277.
PRINCESS AND THE PEA, 1922 Parminter Street, Middleton, Wisconsin 53562.
SALLY S. BOOM, Wildwood Studio, PO Box 303, Montrose, Alabama 36559.

SIGN OF THE ARROW - 1867 FOUNDATION INC, 9740 Clayton Road, St Louis, Missouri 63124.
VILLAGE NEEDLECRAFT INC, 7500 South Memorial Pkwy, Unit 116, Huntsville, Alabama 35802.

Stockists in Canada

DICK AND JANE, 2352 West 41st Avenue, Vancouver, British Columbia V6M 2A4.
FANCYWORKS, 104-3960 Quera Street, Victoria, British Columbia V8X 4A3.
JET HANDCRAFT STUDIO LTD, 1847 Marine Drive, West Vancouver, British Columbia V7V 1J7.
ONE STITCH AT A TIME, PO Box 114, Picton, Ontario K0K 2T0.

Stockists in Australia

CLIFTON H JOSEPH & SON (AUSTRALIA) PTY LTD, 391-393 Little Lonsdale Street, Melbourne, Victoria 3000.
ALTAMIRA, 34 Murphy Street, South Yarra, Melbourne, Victoria 3141.
P L STONEWALL & CO PTY LTD (Flag Division), 52 Erskine Street, Sydney.

Stockists in New Zealand

NANCY'S EMBROIDERY LTD, 326 Tinakori Road, PO Box 245, Thorndon, Wellington.

ANCHOR YARN
U.K.

COATS PATONS CRAFTS, McMullen Road, Darlington, County Durham DL1 1YQ, England. Tel: (0325) 36 54 57.
Fax: (0325) 38 23 00.
U.S.A.
COATS AND CLARK, Susan Bates Inc, 30 Patewood Drive, Greenville, South Carolina 29615. Tel: 1 800 241 5997.
Canada
COATS PATONS CANADA, 1001 Roselawn Avenue, Toronto, Ontario M6B 1B8.
Tel: (416) 782 4481. Toll free: 1 800 268 3620.
Fax: (416) 785 1370.
Australia
COATS PATONS CRAFTS, 89-91 Peters Avenue, Mulgrave, Victoria 3170. Tel: (03) 561 2288.
Fax: (03) 561 2298.
New Zealand
COATS ENZED CRAFTS, East Tamaki, Auckland. Tel: (09) 274 0116.
Fax: (09) 274 0584.

DMC YARN
U.K.
DMC CREATIVE WORLD LTD, Pullman Road, Wigston, Leicestershire LE18 2DY, England.
Tel: (0533) 81 10 40. Fax: (0533) 81 35 92.
U.S.A.
DMC CORPORATION, Building 10, Port Kearny, South Kearny, New Jersey 07032.
Tel: (201) 589 0606. Fax: (201) 589 8931.

Canada see U.S.A.
Australia
DMC NEEDLECRAFT PTY LTD, 51-66 Carrington Road, Marrickville, NSW 2204 or PO Box 317, Earlswood, NSW 2206. Tel: (02) 559 3088.
Fax: (02) 559 5338.

PATERNA/PATERNAYAN YARN
U.K.
PATERNA LTD, PO Box 1, Ossett, West Yorkshire WF5 9SA, England. Tel: (0924) 81 08 12
U.S.A.
PATERNAYAN, JCA INC, 35 Scales Lane, Townsend, Massachusetts 01469.
Tel: (508) 597 8794. Toll free: (800) 225 6340.
Fax: (508) 597 2632.
Australia
ALTAMIRA, 34 Murphy Street, South Yarra, Melbourne. Tel: (3) 867 1240. Fax: (3) 820 34 34.
Canada see U.S.A.
New Zealand
THE STITCHING CO LTD, PO 74-269 Market Road, Auckland. Tel: (09) 366 6080.
Fax: (09) 366 6040.

KREINIK THREADS
U.S.A.
KREINIK, 9199 Resterstown Road, Ste 209B, Owings Mills, Maryland 21117.
Tel: (410) 581 5088. Fax: (410) 581 5092.
U.K. see U.S.A.
Australia
MOSMAN NEEDLECRAFTS, 153 Middlehead Road, Mosman, NSW 2088. Tel: 296 5105.
Canada see U.S.A.
New Zealand
GREVILLE-PARKER, 286 Queen Street, Masterton. Tel: (059) 81 729.

ALICE STARMORE NEEDLEPOINT KITS

The following Alice Starmore needlepoint designs are available as kits with hand painted canvases:

page 14   Key Pattern Cushion
page 22   Key and Knotwork Workbox Cover
page 28   Key and Knotwork Footstool Cover
page 36   Spiral Cushion
page 42   Spiral Chessboard
page 58   Hexagonal Knotwork Cushion
page 64   Knotwork Belt
page 68   Knotwork Carpet Seat Cushion
page 76   Eagle Tile Cushion
page 82   Interlaced Heron Bookmark
page 98   Beast-head Belt
page 108 Lion Tile Cushion

For kit stockists contact:
The Broad Bay Co, PO Box 242, Lambertville, New Jersey 08530-0240, U.S.A.
Tel: (609) 397 9179. Fax: (609) 397 4597.

FURNITURE AND JEWELLERY CREDITS

The buckles on pages 65 and 99 were designed by Alice Starmore. The buckles are available made to order from:
Colin Campbell, Goldsmith, 22 Market Brae, Inverness, Scotland IV2 3AB.
The workbox on page 22, the footstool on page 28 and the stool on page 90 are all available made to order from:
Ian Foster, Cheriton Cottage, Wreningham, Norwich NR16 18E, England.

PICTURE CREDITS

Images Colour Library *6-7, 12-13, 56-57, 74-75, 96-97*
British Museum *9*
Trinity College Dublin *11*
Mick Sharp *34-35*
Rosemary Weller *18-19, 39, 79, 114-115 (Weller photos copyright © Anaya Publishers Ltd 1994)*

ACCESSORIES CREDITS

The stylist Barbara Stewart would like to thank Sarah Jane Stewart for the loan of her beautiful ceramics and Creativity for the loan of yarn and needlework accessories.
SARAH JANE STEWART, 74 Knighthead Point, Isle of Dogs, London E14. Tel: (071) 515 9402.
CREATIVITY, 45 New Oxford Street, London WC1.
The publishers would like to thank the Pastimes shop on Regent Street for extra props.

ACKNOWLEDGEMENTS

I would like to thank everyone involved in the creation of this book. Thanks to Carey Smith of Anaya Publishers, to photographers Rosemary Weller and Jon Stewart, to stylist Barbara Stewart, to chartists Michael Murphy, Stephen Dew and Delia Elliman, and to book designers Ian Muggeridge and Jo Tapper. Very special thanks to my editor Sally Harding for her unswerving support, patience and hard work.